THE PARENT COMPANION

A SUPER HOMEWORK DICTIONARY FOR PARENTS!

DESIGNED FOR STUDENTS
K-12

JONATHAN EDISON, M.ED.

BECAUSE PARENTS SHOULD KNOW WHAT'S GOING ON TOO!

THIS BOOK INCLUDES:
Learning Styles, Language Arts, Mathematics, Science, Social Studies and much, much more...

BONUS: TEXT LANGUAGE

Copyright

Crown Book Publishing
143 Cady Center suite #165
Northville, MI 48167

The Parent Companion: A Super Homework Dictionary for Parents ©2015 by Jonathan Edward Edison. All rights reserved. No part of this book may be used or reproduced in any manner whatsoever without written permission except in the case of brief quotations embodied in critical articles and reviews. For more information contact Crown Publishing Inc.

Manufactured in the United States of America
13 15 17 19 20 18 16 14
First Perennial paper back edition published 2015

Designed by Kendra Cagle

For information about special discounts for bulk purchases, please contact
Edison Speaks International, 1-972-755-4231 or www.jonathanedison.com
or www.theparentcompanion.com

The Library of Congress has catalogued the edition of this book as follows: Edison, Jonathan Edward. The Parent Companion: A Super Homework Dictionary for Parents/by Jonathan Edison - 1st edition Crown Publishing ed.
p. cm.
ISBN 978-1-4951-2475-4 (alk.paper)

All rights reserved

No part of this book may be reproduced or transmitted in any form or by any means, electronic or mechanical, including photocopying, recording, or by any information storage and retrieval system, without expressed written consent of the author and copyright holder.

www.theparentcompanion.com

A SUPER HOMEWORK DICTIONARY FOR PARENTS!

THE PARENT COMPANION

TABLE OF CONTENTS

LEARNING STYLES

Different Learning Styles 5
Visual Learner 8
Auditory Learner 9
Kinstetic Learner 10
Read/Write Learner.................... 11
Learning Preferences 22
Learning Style Inventory 24
Learning Style Assessments 27
Scoring Procedures.................... 30

LANGUAGE ARTS

Abbreviations......................... 34
Adjectives............................ 38
Adverbs.............................. 40
Capitalization 46
Cause & Effect........................ 50
Comma............................... 53
Compounds, subject, sentence 61
Conjuctions 65
Context.............................. 66
Contractions.......................... 69
Digraph.............................. 73
Footnotes............................ 76
Homonym, Homophones, Homographs ... 81

Nouns 83
Outlining 88
Predicates 93
Prefix 95
Prepositions 97
Punctuation 101
Sentences 111
Simile and Metaphor 115
Suffix 125
Topic Sentence 129
Writing Process 133

MATHEMATICS

Addition 136
Subtraction 136
Measurement 149
Mixed Operations 138
Estimating and Rounding 140
Probability 143
Stem and Leaf Plots 145
Graphing 147
Length 150
Mass 152
Volume 155
Time 157
Multiplication 160
Whole Numbers 161

Integers..............................161
Division..............................162
Fractions.............................167
Decimals.............................170
Geometry............................183
Angles...............................184
Shapes..............................191
Math Terms.........................192

SCIENCE

Science Giants (Inventors).............216
Clouds...............................236
Dinosaurs............................237
Rock.................................239
Ice Age..............................243
Weather.............................245
Science Glossary Terms...............246

SOCIAL STUDIES

Amendments.........................265
States and Capitals...................267
Civil Rights Leaders...................269
Presidents and Vice Presidents.........283
Map of the United States..............286
Cardinal Directions...................287
Social Study Glossary Terms...........288

CHAPTER 1

THE 7 LEARNING STYLES:
WHAT ARE THEY?

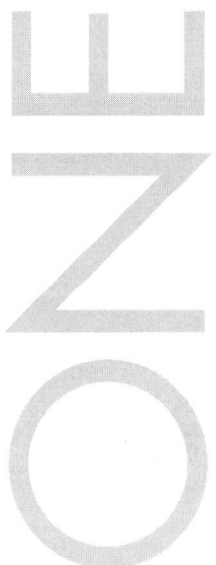

Different Learning Styles in Education

Different people learn differently, and psychologists have attempted through the years to spell out the traits of different types of learners and categorize them into different "learning styles."

Background History
Accounting for individual learning styles in not a new idea. As early as 334 BC, Aristotle said that "each child possessed specific talents and skills" and he noticed individual differences in young children.

In the early 1900's, several personality theories and classifications for individual differences were advanced; these focused especially on the relationship between memory and visual or oral instructional methods. The research in learning styles then declined due to the emphasis on the student's IQ and academic achievement.

In the last half of the 1900's, however, there has been a renewed interest in learning styles research and many educators are attempting to apply the results within the classroom.

Definition of Learning Styles
You have probably noticed that when you try to learn something new you prefer to learn by listening to someone talk to you about the information. Or perhaps you prefer to read about a concept to learn it, or maybe see a demonstration.

Learning styles can be defined, classified, and identified in many different way. Generally, they are overall patterns that provide direction to learning and teaching. Learning style can also be described as a set of factors, behaviors, and attitudes that facilitate learning for an individual in a given situation.

Styles influence how students learn, how teachers teach, and how the two interact. Each person is born with certain tendencies toward particular styles, but these biological or inherited characteristics are influenced by culture, personal experiences, maturity level, and development. Style can be considered a "contextual" variable or construct because what the learner brings to the learning experience is as much a part of the context as are the important features of the experience itself.

Each learner has distinct and consistent preferred ways of perception, organization and retention. These learning styles are characteristic cognitive, affective, and physiological behaviors that serve as pretty good indicators of how learners perceive, interact with, and respond to the learning environment.

Students learn differently from each other and it has been determined that brain structure influences language structure acquisition. It has also been shown that different hemispheres of the brain contain different perception avenues. Some researchers claim that several types of cells present in some brains are not present in others.

LET'S EXPLORE!

Visual Learning Style

People with a visual learning style absorb information by seeing it in front of them and storing the images in their brains. They often enjoy reading, have good handwriting, are very detail-oriented, are organized, and have a keen awareness of colors and shapes.

They tend to struggle with verbal directions and are easily distracted by noise. They remember people's faces better than their names, and they often need to maintain eye contact with a person to concentrate on a conversation.

Here are some tips for helping visual learners excel in the classroom:

- Write out directions.
- Use visuals when teaching lessons, such as pictures, charts, diagrams, maps, and outlines.
- Physically demonstrate tasks.
- Use visual aids such as flashcards and blocks.
- Show the visual patterns in language to teach spelling, vocabulary, grammar, and punctuation.
- Organize information using color codes.
- Talk with the child face-to-face and make eye contact whenever possible.

- When directions are given verbally, encourage the child to ask for clarification when she doesn't understand fully.

- Encourage the child to write plenty of notes and organize information on paper and with objects.

- Provide a quiet, neat place to study, and minimize distractions as much as possible.

Auditory Learning Style

Verbal language is the prime form for exchanging information for those within the auditory learning style. They learn best by hearing and speaking. They often talk more than the average person, are very social, enjoy hearing stories and jokes, understand concepts by talking about them, and may excel in music or the performing arts.

Some auditory learners read slowly and have trouble writing, struggle to follow written directions, and have a tough time staying quiet for long stretches of time. They remember names and recognize tone of voice well, while not always remembering people's faces. They often hum or sing, and they may whisper to themselves while reading.

Try these techniques when teaching auditory learners:

- Play word games and use rhymes to practice language.

- Have the child read aloud, even when alone, and follow the text with her finger.

- Allow the child to explain concepts verbally and give oral reports.

- Have the child memorize information by repeating it aloud.

- Assign projects and study times to be done in small and large groups.

- Read aloud often to young children.

- Provide a personal voice recorder the child can use to record notes or questions.

- Use beats, rhythms, and songs to reinforce educational information.

Kinesthetic Learning Style

People with the kinesthetic learning style learn best by doing: moving around and handling physical objects. They like to explore the outdoors, are often very coordinated, may excel in athletics and performing arts, and usually express their feelings physically, such as with hugging and hitting. They prefer trying new skills for themselves rather than being given directions or shown a demonstration.

They may find it hard to sit still for long periods of time and struggle with reading and spelling. They are often considered "difficult" and misdiagnosed with ADHD (attention deficit hyperactivity disorder). In recent years, more educators have accepted that they simply learn differently and have urged educators to consider more kinesthetic learning activities.

These teaching tips can help you get the most out of kinesthetic learners:

- Give breaks frequently.

- Let the child try something first before you give detailed instructions.

- Provide plenty of hands-on learning tools, such as crayons, blocks, puzzles, maps, modeling clay, science experiments, an abacus, and a geoboard (a square board with pegs used to teach shapes and geometric concepts).

- Don't limit the study space to the usual desk. Allow the child to study while moving around, lying on the floor, or slouching in a couch.

- Use the outdoors for learning opportunities.

- Teach educational concepts through games and projects.

- Assign presentations in which children demonstrate concepts or skills.

- Encourage physical movement while studying. For example, quiz the child while taking a walk around the block.

- Find a school with mandatory physical education. Kinesthetic learners suffer most from the recent cutting of P.E. in many schools.

Read/Write Learning Style

The read/write learning style was added to Fleming's model after the initial three. Read/write learners specifically learn best through the written word. They absorb information by reading books and handouts, taking lots of notes (sometimes word-for-word), and making lists. They prefer lectures, diagrams, pictures, charts, and scientific concepts to be explained using written language. They are often fast readers and skillful writers.

Similar to visual learners, read/write learners may struggle with verbal directions and are easily distracted by noise. Some may be quiet and struggle to detect body language and other social cues.

Here are some ways to help read/write learners succeed:

- Encourage the child to write plenty of notes, rewrite them in her own words, and study from them.

- Provide thorough, well-organized written material, and write key points in full sentences on the board during lectures.

- Assign plenty of writing exercises.

- Explain diagrams, graphs, or any mathematical data using language.

- Set up a quiet study area with as few distractions as possible.

- Provide a dictionary, thesaurus, and other resource material.

- Allow the child to answer multiple-choice questions.

The Complexities of Learning Styles

Many other models for learning styles exist, most notably David Kolb's Experiential Learning Model and Learning Style Inventory, which are used to categorize adults more so than children.

Whichever model of learning styles is used, psychologists agree that almost no one falls neatly into only one learning style. People may be categorized into one, but their various traits can apply to others—or they may have a secondary learning style that works for them significantly better than another. For example, a student may be primarily a visual learner, have some skills for auditory learning, and have no skill for learning kinesthetically.

Additionally, some psychologists have proposed that all children are primarily kinesthetic learners until second or third grade, only developing other learning styles when their education becomes more rigorous.

Modality:
VISUAL LEARNERS (INPUT)

Descriptors:
- Learn by observation
- Can recall what they have seen
- Can follow written or drawn instructions
- Like to read
- Use written notes
- Benefit by visualizing, watching TV/video/films

Learn Best Through the Use of:
- Charts, graphs, diagrams, and flow charts
- Sight words
- Flashcards
- Visual similarities and differences
- Pictures and graphics
- Maps
- Silent reading
- Written instructions
- Computer assisted learning

Modality:
AUDITORY LEARNERS (INPUT) VERBAL-LINGUISTIC INTELLIGENCE

Descriptors:
- Prefer listening and taking notes
- Listen for patterns
- Consult peers to ascertain that they have the correct details
- Can recall what they have heard
- Can follow oral directions
- Repeat words aloud for memorizartion
- Use oral language effectively

Learn Best Through the Use of:
- Discussion, dialog, debate
- Memorization
- Phonics
- Oral reading
- Hearing anecdotes or stories
- Listening to tapes or CDs
- Cooperartive learning groups

Modality:
KINESTHETIC LEARNERS (INPUT)

Descriptors:
- Are often physically adept
- Learn through experience and physical activity
- Benefit from demonstration
- Learn from teaching others what they know

Learn Best Through the Use of:
- Playing games
- Role playing
- Read body language/gestures
- Mime
- Drama
- Learn or memorize while moving *(pacing, stationary bike, finger or whole body games)*

Modality:
TACTILE LEARNERS (INPUT)

Descriptors:
- Learn by touching and manipulating objects
- Often learn inductively rather than deductively
- Tend toward pscychomotor over abstract thinking
- Prefer personal connections to topics
- Follow directions they have written themselves / that they have rehearsed
- Benefit from demonstrations

Learn Best Through the Use of:
- Learning by doing
- "Hands-on"
- Creating maps
- Building models
- Art projects
- Using manipulatives
- Drawing, designing things
- Writing / tracing

Modality:
ACTIVE

Descriptors:
- Can be impulsive
- Risk-takers
- Do not prefer lectures
- Prefer group work
- Tend to be interpersonal
- Not inclined to too much note-taking

Learn Best Through the Use of:
- Prefer "doing, discussin, explaining" vs listening and watching
- Prefer active experimentation
- Like acting and role playing
- Like team competition

Modality:
REFLECTIVE

Descriptors:
- Prefer to think about concepts quietly before any action
- Learn by thinking
- Like writing
- Tend to be intrapersonal and introspective

Learn Best Through the Use of:
- Tend toward deductive learning
- Prefer reflective observation
- Intrapersonal skills valued
- Journals
- Learning logs

Modality:
GLOBAL UNDERSTANDING

Descriptors:
- Make decisions based on intuition
- Spontaneous and creative; "idea" person
- Often a risk-taker
- Tend to reach conclusions quickly
- Intake information in large chunks rather than details
- Nonlinear thinkers
- "See the forest before they see the trees."

Learn Best Through the Use of:
- Interpersonal connection important to them
- Stories and anecdotes
- Seeing the "whole" rather than in parts
- Highly interesting project and materials
- Functional games and activities
- Think-pair-share; Praise-question-polish
- Teacher feedback; person-to-person communication

Modality:
ANALYTICAL UNDERSTANDING

Descriptors:

- Sequential, linear learners
- Prefer information in small chumks, steps
- Can follow the rules for mathematic equations
- Prefer a logical progression
- "See the trees before they see the forest."

Learn Best Through the Use of:

- Intrapersonal skills valued
- Journals
- Learning logs
- Sequentially organized material, timelines, diagrams
- Moving from "part" to the "whole"
- Puzzles, logic games

Learning Preferences

Field Dependent Definition:
[field sensitive] - tends toward concrete: more teacher and group interaction

Field Independent Definition:
tends toward abstract

Field Dependent Learner

- Experiences in a global fashion, adheres to structures
- Learns material with social content best
- Attends best to material relevant to own experience
- Requires externally defined goals and reinforcements
- Needs organization provided
- More affected by criticism
- Uses observational approach for concept attainment [learns best by using examples]

Field Dependent Teaching Styles

- Prefers teaching situations that allow interaction and discussion with students
- Uses questions to check on student learning following instruction
- Uses student-centered activities
- Viewed by students as teaching facts
- Provides less feedback, positive feedback

- Strong in establishing a warm and personal learning environment

Field Independent Learners
- Perceives analytically
- Makes specific concept distinctions; little overlap
- Impersonal orientation
- May need explicit training in social skills
- Interested in new concepts for their own sake
- Has self-defined goals and reinforcement
- Can self-structure situations
- Less affected by criticism
- Uses hypothesis-testing approach to attain concepts

Field Independent Teaching Styles
- Prefers engaging students by establishing routines in order to work through ideas
- Uses questions to introduce topics and probe student answers
- Uses teacher-organized learning situations
- Viewed by students as encouraging to apply principles
- Gives corrective feedback using error analysis
- Strong in organizing and guiding student learning

Learning Styles Assessment

Read each statement and select the appropriate number response as it applies to you.

OFTEN = 3 points
SOMETIMES = 2 points
SELDOM = 1 point

Visual Modality

____ I remember information better if I write it down.

____ Looking at the person helps keep me focused.

____ I need a quiet place to get my work done.

____ When I take a test, I can see the textbook page in my head.

____ I need to write down directions, not just take them verbally.

____ Music or background noise distracts my attention from the task at hand.

____ I don't always get the meaning of a joke.

____ I doodle and draw pictures on the margins of my notebook pages.

____ I have trouble following lectures.

____ I react very strongly to colors.

____ TOTAL

Auditory Modality

____ My papers and notebooks always seem messy.

____ When I read, I need to use my index finger to track my place on the line.

____ I do not follow written directions well.

____ If I hear something, I will remember it.

____ Writing has always been difficult for me.

____ I often misread words from the text (i.e., "them" for "then").

____ I would rather listen and learn than read and learn.

____ I'm not very good at interpreting an individual's body language.

____ Pages with small print or poor quality copies are difficult for me to read.

____ My eyes tire quickly, even though my vision check-up is always fine.

____ TOTAL

Kinesthetic/Tactile Modality

____ I start a project before reading the directions.

____ I hate to sit at a desk for long periods of time.

____ I prefer first to see something done and then to do it myself.

____ I use the trial and error approach to problem-solving.

____ I like to read my textbook while riding an exercise bike.

____ I take frequent study breaks.

____ I have a difficult time giving step-by-step instructions.
____ I enjoy sports and do well at several different types of sports.
____ I use my hands when describing things.
____ I have to rewrite or type my class notes to reinforce the material.
____ TOTAL

Total the score for each section.

A score of 21 points or more in a modality indicates a strength in that area. The highest of the 3 scores indicates the most efficient method of information intake. The second highest score indicates the modality which boosts the primary strength. For example, a score of 23 in visual modality indicates a strong visual learner. Such a learner benefits from the text, from filmstrips, charts, graphs, etc. If the second highest score is auditory, then the individual would benefit from audio tapes, lectures, etc. If you are strong kinesthetically, then taking notes and rewriting class notes will reinforce information.

Learning Style Inventory

To better understand how you prefer to learn and process information, place a check in the appropriate space after each statement below, then use the scoring directions at the bottom of the page to evaluate your responses. Use what you learn from your scores to better develop learning strategies that are best suited to your particular learning style.

This 24-item survey is not timed. Respond to each statement as honestly as you can.

		ALWAYS	SOMETIMES	SELDOM
1.	I can remember best about a subject by listening to a lecture that includes information, explanations and discussions.			
2.	I prefer to see information written on a chalkboard and supplemented by visual aids and assigned readings.			
3.	I like to write things down or to take notes for visual review.			
4.	I prefer to use posters, models, or actual practice and other activities in class.			
5.	I require explanations of diagrams, graphs, or visual directions.			

		ALWAYS	SOMETIMES	SELDOM
6.	I enjoy working with my hands or making things.			
7.	I am skillful with and enjoy developing and making graphs and charts.			
8.	I can tell if sounds match when presented with pairs of sounds.			
9.	I can remember best by writing things down.			
10.	I can easily understand and follow directions on a map.			
11.	I do best in academic subjects by listening to lectures and tapes.			
12.	I play with coins or keys in my pocket.			
13.	I learn to spell better by repeating words out loud than by writing the words on paper.			
14.	I can understand a news article better by reading about it in a newspaper than by listening to a report about it on the radio.			
15.	I chew gum, smoke or snack while studying.			
16.	I think the best way to remember something is to picture it in your head.			

	ALWAYS	SOMETIMES	SELDOM
17. I learn the spelling of words by "finger spelling" them.			
18. I would rather listen to a good lecture or speech than read about the same material in a textbook.			
19. I am good at working and solving jigsaw puzzles and mazes.			
20. I grip objects in my hands during learning periods.			
21. I prefer listening to the news on the radio rather than reading the paper.			
22. I prefer obtaining information about an interesting subject by reading about it.			
23. I feel very comfortable touching others, hugging, hand-shaking, etc.			
24. I follow oral directions better than written ones.			

Scoring Procedures

Directions: Place the point value on the line next to the corresponding item below. Add the points in each column to obtain the preference score under each heading.

OFTEN = 5 points
SOMETIMES = 3 points
SELDOM = 1 point

VISUAL		AUDITORY		TACTILE	
NO.	PTS.	NO.	PTS.	NO.	PTS.
2		1		2	
3		5		3	
7		8		7	
10		11		10	
14		13		14	
16		18		16	
19		21		19	
22		24		22	
VPS =		APS =		VPS =	

VPS = Visual Preference
APS = Audio Preference
TPS = Tactile Preference

If you are a VISUAL learner, by all means be sure that you look at all study materials. Use charts, maps, filmstrips, notes, videos, and flash cards. Practice visualizing or picturing words and concepts in your head. Write out everything for frequent and quick visual review.

If you are an AUDITORY learner, you may wish to use tapes. Tape lectures to help fill in gaps in your notes. But do listen and take notes - and review your notes frequently. Sit in the lecture hall or classroom where you can hear well. After you have read something, summarize it and recite it aloud. Talk to other students about class material.

If you are a TACTILE learner, trace words as you are saying them. Facts that must be learned should be written several times. Keep a supply of scratch paper on hand for this purpose. Taking and keeping lecture notes is very important. Make study sheets. Associate class material with real-world things or occurrences. When appropriate, practice role playing.

RESULTS:

How does your child learn?_____

What's your child's Learning Style Test?_____

How do you learn as a Parent? _____

What did you discover about your child?

_____
_____
_____
_____
_____
_____
_____
_____
_____
_____
_____
_____
_____
_____

THE PARENT COMPANION
A SUPER HOMEWORK DICTIONARY FOR PARENTS!

CHAPTER 2
LANGUAGE **ARTS**

lan·guage arts
noun

noun: language arts; plural noun: language artses
the study of grammar, composition, spelling, and (sometimes) public speaking, typically taught as a single subject in elementary and middle school.

Abbreviations

Shortened form of a word usually beginning with a capital letter and sometimes ending with a period. Some words that can be abbreviated are: titles, words used in addresses words used in business, states, proper names, and words that have capital letters in their title.

EXAMPLES:
State Abbreviations

AK	Alaska	**MT**	Montana
AL	Alabama	**NC**	North Carolina
AR	Arkansas	**ND**	North Dakota
AZ	Arizona	**NE**	Nebraska
CA	California	**NH**	New Hampshire
CO	Colorado	**NJ**	New Jersey
CT	Connecticut	**NM**	New Mexico
DC	District of Columbia	**NV**	Nevada
DE	Delaware	**NY**	New York
FL	Florida	**OH**	Ohio
GA	Georgia	**OK**	Oklahoma
HI	Hawaii	**OR**	Oregon
IA	Iowa	**PA**	Pennsylvania
ID	Idaho	**RI**	Rhode Island
IL	Illinois	**SC**	South Carolina
IN	Indiana	**SD**	South Dakota
KS	Kansas	**TN**	Tennessee
KY	Kentucky	**TX**	Texas
LA	Louisiana	**UT**	Utah
MA	Massachusetts	**VA**	Virginia
MD	Maryland	**VT**	Vermont
ME	Maine	**WA**	Washington
MI	Michigan	**WI**	Wisconsin
MN	Minnesota	**WV**	West Virginia
MO	Missouri	**WY**	Wyoming
MS	Mississippi		

Common Informative Abbreviations

DOA	Dead On Arrival
AIDS	Acquired Immune Deficiency Syndrome
HIV	Human Immunodeficiency Virus
DARE	Drug Abuse Resistance Education
ADD	Attention Deficit Disorder
ADHD	Attention Deficit Hyperactivity Disorder
DOB	Date Of Birth
OTC	Over The Counter
CDC	Centers for Disease Control and Prevention
ASAP	As Soon As Possible
FYI	For Your Information
EST	Eastern Standard Time
PST	Pacific Standard Time
CST	Central Standard Time
PPV	Pay Per View
SSN	Social Security Number
JIT	Just In Time
ADL	Activities of Daily Living
AMA	Against Medical Advice
MD	Medical Doctor

Common abbreviations for identity

NFL	National Football League
AFL	American Football League
NBA	National Basketball Association
NHL	National Hockey League
AA	Alcoholics Anonymous
AARP	American Association of Retired Persons
MADD	Mothers Against Drunk Driving
PGA	Professional Golfer's Association
APA	American Psychological Association
ACS	American Cancer Society

AMA	American Medical Association
ADA	American Dental Association
AA	African American
AKA	Also Known As
DBA	Doing Business As
DND	Do Not Disturb
MBA	Masters of Business Administration
OT	Overtime
POS	Point Of Service
DAEMON	Disk And Execution Monitor
HR	Human Resources
POP	Post Office Protocol
TNT	Tuner Network Television
TBC	To Be Continued
TBN	Trinity Broadcasting Network
ESPN	Entertainment and Sports Programming Network
CBS	Columbia Broadcasting System
MTV	Music Television
NBC	National Broadcasting Company
ABS	Anti-lock Breaking System
ABC	American Broadcasting Company
PBS	Public Broadcasting Service
UFO	Unidentified Flying Object

Adjectives

A word used to describe a noun or pronoun. Adjectives tell what kind, how many or which one.

EXAMPLES:

Appearance Adjectives
Adorable, beautiful, clean, drab, elegant, fancy, glamorous, handsome, long, magnificent, old-fashioned, plain, quaint, sparkling, ugliest, unsightly, wide-eyed

Condition Adjectives
Alive, better, careful, clever, dead, easy, famous, gifted, helpful, important, inexpensive, mushy, odd, powerful, rich, shy, tender, uninterested, vast, wrong

Feelings (Bad) Adjectives
Angry, bewildered, clumsy, defeated, embarrassed, fierce, grumpy, helpless, itchy, jealous, lazy, mysterious, nervous, obnoxious, panicky, repulsive, scary, thoughtless, uptight, worried

Feelings (Good) Adjectives
Agreeable, brave, calm, delightful, eager, faithful, gentle, happy, jolly, kind, lively, nice, obedient, proud, relieved, silly, thankful, victorious, witty, zealous

Size Adjectives
Big, colossal, fat, gigantic, great, huge, immense, large, little, mammoth, massive, miniature, petite, puny, scrawny, short, small, tall, teeny, teeny-tiny

Sound Adjectives
Cooing, deafening, faint, hissing, loud, melodic, noisy, purring, quiet, raspy, screeching, thundering, voiceless, whispering

Time Adjectives
Ancient, brief, early, fast, late, long, modern, old-fashioned, quick, rapid, short, slow, swift, young

Adverbs

Word that describes a verb and sometimes ends in –ly. Adverbs tell you when, how, how much, or where an action happens.

A
abnormally
absentmindedly
accidentally
acidly
actually
adventurously
afterwards
almost
always
angrily
annually
anxiously
arrogantly
awkwardly

B
badly
bashfully
beautifully
bitterly
bleakly
blindly
blissfully
boastfully
boldly
bravely
briefly
brightly
briskly
broadly
busily

C
calmly
carefully
carelessly
cautiously
certainly
cheerfully
clearly
cleverly
closely
coaxingly
colorfully
commonly
continually
coolly
correctly
courageously
crossly
cruelly
curiously

D
daily
daintily
dearly

deceivingly
delightfully
deeply
defiantly
deliberately
delightfully
diligently
dimly
doubtfully
dreamily

E

easily
elegantly
energetically
enormously
enthusiastically
equally
especially
even
evenly
eventually
exactly
excitedly
extremely

F

fairly
faithfully
famously
far
fast
fatally
ferociously
fervently

fiercely
fondly
foolishly
fortunately
frankly
frantically
freely
frenetically
frightfully
fully
furiously

G

generally
generously
gently
gladly
gleefully
gracefully
gratefully
greatly
greedily

H

happily
hastily
healthily
heavily
helpfully
helplessly
highly
honestly
hopelessly
hourly
hungrily

I

immediately
innocently
inquisitively
instantly
intensely
intently
interestingly
inwardly
irritably

J

jaggedly
jealously
joshingly
joyfully
joyously
jovially
jubilantly
judgementally
justly

K

keenly
kiddingly
kindheartedly
kindly
kissingly
knavishly
knottily
knowingly
knowledgeably
kookily

L

lazily
less
lightly
likely
limply
lively
loftily
longingly
loosely
lovingly
loudly
loyally

M

madly
majestically
meaningfully
mechanically
merrily
miserably
mockingly
monthly
more
mortally
mostly
mysteriously

N

naturally
nearly
neatly
needily
nervously

never
nicely
noisily
not

O

obediently
obnoxiously
oddly
offensively
officially
often
only
openly
optimistically
overconfidently
owlishly

P

painfully
partially
patiently
perfectly
physically
playfully
politely
poorly
positively
potentially
powerfully
promptly
properly
punctually

Q

quaintly
quarrelsomely
queasily
queerly
questionably
questioningly
quicker
quickly
quietly
quirkily
quizzically

R

rapidly
rarely
readily
really
reassuringly
recklessly
regularly
reluctantly
repeatedly
reproachfully
restfully
righteously
rightfully
rigidly
roughly
rudely

S

sadly
safely

scarcely
scarily
searchingly
sedately
seemingly
seldom
selfishly
separately
seriously
shakily
sharply
sheepishly
shrilly
shyly
silently
sleepily
slowly
smoothly
softly
solemnly
solidly
sometimes
soon
speedily
stealthily
sternly
strictly
successfully
suddenly
surprisingly
suspiciously
sweetly
swiftly
sympathetically

T

tenderly
tensely
terribly
thankfully
thoroughly
thoughtfully
tightly
tomorrow
too
tremendously
triumphantly
truly
truthfully

U

ultimately
unabashedly
unaccountably
unbearably
unethically
unexpectedly
unfortunately
unimpressively
unnaturally
unnecessarily
utterly
upbeat
upliftingly
upright
upside-down
upward
upwardly
urgently
usefully

uselessly
usually
utterly

V

vacantly
vaguely
vainly
valiantly
vastly
verbally
very
viciously
victoriously
violently
vivaciously
voluntarily

W

warmly
weakly
wearily
well
wetly
wholly
wildly
willfully
wisely
woefully
wonderfully
worriedly
wrongly

Y

yawningly
yearly
yearningly
yesterday
yieldingly
youthfully

Z

zealously
zestfully
zestily

Capitalization

Capitalization Rules

Capitalization is the writing of a word with its first letter in uppercase and the remaining letters in lowercase. Experienced writers are stingy with capitals. It is best not to use them if there is any doubt.

RULE 1.
Capitalize the first word of a document and the first word after a period.

RULE 2.
Capitalize proper nouns—and adjectives derived from proper nouns.

EXAMPLES:
*the Golden Gate Bridge, the Grand Canyon,
a Russian song, a Shakespearean sonnet,
a Freudian slip*

With the passage of time, some words originally derived from proper nouns have taken on a life, and authority, of their own and no longer require capitalization.

EXAMPLES:
herculean (from the ancient-Greek hero Hercules)
quixotic (from the hero of the classic novel Don Quixote) *draconian* (from ancient-Athenian lawgiver Draco)

The main function of capitals is to focus attention on particular elements within any group of people, places, or things. We can speak of a lake in the middle of the country, or we can be more specific and say Lake Michigan, which distinguishes it from every other lake on earth.

Capitalization Reference List

- Brand names
- Companies
- Days of the week and months of the year
- Governmental matters - *Congress* (but *congressional*), *the U.S. Constitution* (but *constitutional*), *the Electoral College, Department of Agriculture*. **Note:** Many authorities do not capitalize *federal* or *state* unless it is part of the official title - *State Water Resources Control Board,* but *state water board; Federal Communications Commission,* but *federal regulations.*
- Historical episodes and eras *the Inquisition, the American Revolutionary War, the Great Depression*
- Holidays
- Institutions - *Oxford College, the Juilliard School of Music*
- Manmade structures - *the Empire State Building, the Eiffel Tower, the Titanic*
- Manmade territories - *Berlin, Montana, Cook County*
- Natural and manmade landmarks - *Mount Everest, the Hoover Dam*

- Nicknames and epithets - *Andrew "Old Hickory" Jackson; Babe Ruth, the Sultan of Swat*
- Organizations - *American Center for Law and Justice, Norwegian Ministry of the Environment*
- Planets - *Mercury, Venus, Mars, Jupiter, Saturn, Uranus, Neptune,* but policies vary on capitalizing *earth,* and it is usually not capitalized unless it is being discussed specifically as a planet: *We learned that Earth travels through space at 66,700 miles per hour.*
- Races, nationalities, and tribes - *Eskimo, Navajo, East Indian, Caucasian, African American* (**Note:** *white* and *black* in reference to race are lowercase)
- Religions and names of deities **Note:** Capitalize *the Bible* (but *biblical*). Do not capitalize *heaven, hell, the devil, satanic.*
- Special occasions - *the Olympic Games, the Cannes Film Festival*
- Streets and roads

Lowercase Reference List

Here is a list of categories *not* capitalized unless an item contains a proper noun or proper adjective (or, sometimes, a trademark). In such cases, only the proper noun or adjective is capitalized.

- Animals - *antelope, black bear, Bengal tiger, yellow-bellied sapsucker, German shepherd*
- Elements: Always lowercase, even when the name is derived from a proper noun: *einsteinium, nobelium, californium*

- Foods: Lowercase except for brand names, proper nouns and adjectives, or custom-named recipes - *Tabasco sauce, Russian dressing, pepper crusted bluefin tuna, Mandy's Bluefin Surprise*
- Heavenly bodies besides planets. Never capitalize the *moon* or the *sun*.
- Medical conditions - *Epstein-Barr syndrome, tuberculosis, Parkinson's disease*
- Minerals
- Plants, vegetables, and fruits - *poinsettia, Douglas fir, Jerusalem artichoke, organic celery, Golden Delicious apples*
- Seasons and seasonal data - *spring, summertime, the winter solstice, the autumnal equinox, daylight saving time*

RULE 3.

A thorny aspect of capitalization: where does it stop? When does the *Iraq war* become the *Iraq War*? Why is the legendary *Hope Diamond* not the *Hope diamond*? Everyone writes *New York City*, so why does the *Associated Press Stylebook* recommend *New York state*? There aren't always easy formulas or logical explanations. Research with reference books and search engines is the best strategy.

In the case of brand names, companies are of little help, because they capitalize any word that applies to their merchandise. *Domino's Pizza* or *Domino's pizza*? Is it *Ivory Soap* or *Ivory soap*, a *Hilton Hotel* or a *Hilton hotel*? Most writers don't capitalize common nouns that simply describe the products *(pizza, soap, hotel)*, but it's not always easy to determine where a brand name ends. There is *Time* magazine but also the *New York Times Magazine*. No one would argue with *Coca-Cola* or *Pepsi Cola*, but a case could be made for *Royal Crown cola*.

If a trademark starts with a lowercase word or letter *(e.g., eBay, iPhone)*, many authorities advise capitalizing it to begin a sentence.

EXAMPLE:
EBay opened strong in trading today.

Cause & Effect

Cause and Effect Examples
Cause and effect is a relationship between events or things, where one is the result of the other or others. This is a combination of action and reaction.

EXAMPLES:
- **We received seven inches of rain in four hours.** - The underpass was flooded.
- **I never brush my teeth.** - I have 5 cavities.
- **Smoking cigarettes** - Lung cancer
- **Many buffalo were killed.** - Buffalo almost became extinct.
- **The streets were snow-packed and icy.** - Cars needed more time to stop.
- **He broke his arm.** - The doctor put it in a cast.
- **The boss was busy.** - Her secretary took a message.
- **A basketball player was traveling.** - The referee called a penalty.

- **I flipped the light switch on.** - The light came on.
- **An oil spill** - Many deaths to wildlife
- **Sedentary lifestyle** - Childhood obesity

Cause and Effect Examples in Sentences

- When water is heated, the molecules move quickly, therefore the water boils.
- A tornado blew the roof off the house, and as a result, the family had to find another place to live.
- Because the alarm was not set, we were late for work.
- The moon has gravitational pull, consequently the oceans have tides.
- Since school was canceled, we went to the mall.
- John made a rude comment, so Elise hit him.
- When the ocean is extremely polluted, coral reefs die.
- The meal we ordered was cheaper than expected, so we ordered dessert.
- Since helium rises, a helium balloon floats.
- There has been an increase in greenhouse gases, therefore global warming is happening.
- Betty completed each task perfectly, therefore she was promoted.
- Some believe dinosaurs died out because a large meteor hit the earth.

- I had to get the mop since I spilled my juice.
- Tsunamis happen when tectonic plates shift.
- Fred was driving 75 in a 35 mile zone, therefore he got a speeding ticket.
- Because of changes in classifications, Pluto is no longer a planet.
- Maria didn't follow the recipe correctly, so the cake did not come out as expected.
- The weather forecast called for rain, so he took his umbrella.
- Because of a price increase, sales are down.
- Water is formed when two hydrogen atoms and one oxygen atom combine.
- The baby was crying, so Dad picked him up.
- I learned to play the drums quickly because I took lessons from a pro.
- The batter couldn't hit the softball because he didn't keep his eyes on the ball.
- When the manuscript is edited, the company will publish it.
- Because the cat was frightened, he arched his back and fluffed his tail.
- A peacock will spread his feathers so he will attract a female.
- Since the electricity went out for most of the day, the ice cream in the freezer melted.
- As the wind speed increases, the sail boat moves faster.
- When nuclear fusion stops or starts, a star explodes.

- Wind is produced when the surface of the Earth is heated unevenly.
- Because of inflation, the dollar is worth less than before.
- Since the refrigerator was practically empty, we had to go to the store.

Comma

RULE 1.
Use a comma **to separate the elements in a series** (three or more things), including the last two. "He hit the ball, dropped the bat, and ran to first base." You may have learned that the comma before the "and" is unnecessary, which is fine if you're in control of things. However, there are situations in which, if you don't use this comma (especially when the list is complex or lengthy), these last two items in the list will try to glom together (like macaroni and cheese). Using a comma between *all the items in a series, including the last two,* avoids this problem. This last comma—the one between the word "and" and the preceding word—is often called the **serial comma** or the **Oxford comma.** In newspaper writing, incidentally, you will seldom find a serial comma, but that is not necessarily a sign that it should be omitted in academic prose.

RULE 2.
Use a comma + a little conjunction (and, but, for, nor, yet, or, so) **to connect two independent clauses,** as in "He hit the ball well, *but* he ran toward third base."

Contending that the coordinating conjunction is adequate separation, some writers will leave out the comma in a sentence with short, balanced independent clauses (such as we see in the example just given). If there is ever any doubt, however, use the comma, as it is always correct in this situation.

One of the most frequent errors in comma usage is the placement of a comma after a coordinating conjunction. We cannot say that the comma will always come before the conjunction and never *after,* but it would be a rare event, indeed, that we need to follow a coordinating conjunction with a comma. When speaking, we do sometimes pause after the little conjunction, but there is seldom a good reason to put a comma there.

RULE # 3
Use a comma **to set off introductory elements,** as in *"Running toward third base,* he suddenly realized how stupid he looked."

It is permissible to omit the comma after a brief introductory element if the omission does not result in confusion or hesitancy in reading. If there is ever any doubt, use the comma, as it is always correct.

RULE # 4
Use a comma **to set off parenthetical elements,** as in "The Founders Bridge, *which spans the Connecticut River,* is falling down." By "parenthetical element," we mean a part of a sentence that can be removed without changing the essential meaning of that sentence. The parenthetical element is sometimes called "added information." This is the most difficult

rule in punctuation because it is sometimes unclear what is "added" or "parenthetical" and what is essential to the meaning of a sentence.

Appositives are almost always treated as parenthetical elements.

- Calhoun's ambition, *to become a goalie in professional soccer,* is within his reach.
- Eleanor, *his wife of thirty years,* suddenly decided to open her own business.

Sometimes the appositive and the word it identifies are so closely related that the comma can be omitted, as in "His wife Eleanor suddenly decided to open her own business." We could argue that the name "Eleanor" is not essential to the meaning of the sentence (assuming he has only one wife), and that would suggest that we can put commas both before and after the name (and that would, indeed, be correct). But "his wife" and "Eleanor" are so close that we can regard the entire phrase as one unit and leave out the commas. With the phrase turned around, however, we have a more definite parenthetical element and the commas are necessary: "Eleanor, his wife, suddenly decided to open her own business." Consider, also, the difference between "College President Ira Rubenzahl voted to rescind the withdrawal policy" (in which we need the name "Ira Rubenzahl" or the sentence doesn't make sense) and "Ira Rubenzahl, the college president, voted to rescind the withdrawal policy" (in which the sentence makes sense without his title, the appositive, and we treat the appositive as a parenthetical element, with a pair of commas) When a parenthetical element — an interjection, adverbial modifier, or even an adverbial clause — follows a coordinating conjunction used to connect two independent clauses, we do not put a comma in front of the parenthetical element.

- The Red Sox were leading the league at the end of May, but of course, they always do well in the spring. [no comma after "but"]

- The Yankees didn't do so well in the early going, but frankly, everyone expects them to win the season. [no comma after "but"]

- The Tigers spent much of the season at the bottom of the league, and even though they picked up several promising rookies, they expect to be there again next year.
  [no comma after "and"]

When both a city's name and that city's state or country's name are mentioned together, the state or country's name is treated as a parenthetical element.

- We visited Hartford, Connecticut, last summer.

- Paris, France, is sometimes called "The City of Lights."

- When the state becomes a possessive form, this rule is no longer followed:

- Hartford, Connecticut's investment in the insurance industry is well known.

Also, when the state or country's name becomes part of a compound structure, the second comma is dropped:

- Heublein, a Hartford, Connecticut-based company, is moving to another state.

An **absolute phrase** is always treated as a parenthetical element, as is an **interjection**. An **addressed person's name** is also always parenthetical. Be sure, however, that the name is that of someone actually being spoken to. A separate section on **Vocatives,** the various forms that a parenthetical element related to an addressed person's name can take, is also available.

- *Their years of training now forgotten,* the soldiers broke ranks.
- *Yes,* it is always a matter, *of course,* of preparation and attitude.
- I'm telling you, *Juanita,* I couldn't be more surprised. (I told Juanita I couldn't be more surprised. [no commas])

RULE #5
Use a comma to **separate coordinate adjectives**. You could think of this as "That tall, distinguished, good looking fellow" rule (as opposed to "the little old lady"). If you can put an *and* or a *but* between the adjectives, a comma will probably belong there. For instance, you could say, "He is a tall and distinguished fellow" or "I live in a very old and run-down house." So you would write, "He is a tall, distinguished man"

and "I live in a very old, run-down house." But you would probably not say, "She is a little and old lady," or "I live in a little and purple house," so commas would not appear between *little* and *old* or between *little* and *purple*.

RULE #6

Use a comma **to set off quoted elements.** Because we don't use quoted material all the time, even when writing, this is probably the most difficult rule to remember in comma usage. It is a good idea to find a page from an article that uses several quotations, photocopy that page, and keep it in front of you as a model when you're writing. Generally, use a comma to separate quoted material from the rest of the sentence that explains or introduces the quotation:

- Summing up this argument, Peter Coveney writes, "The purpose and strength of the romantic image of the child had been above all to establish a relation between childhood and adult consciousness."

- If an attribution of a quoted element comes in the middle of the quotation, two commas will be required. But be careful not to create a comma splice in so doing.

- "The question is," said Alice, "whether you can make words mean so many things."

- "I should like to buy an egg, please," she said timidly. "How do you sell them?"

- Be careful *not* to use commas to set off quoted elements introduced by the word *that* or quoted elements that are embedded in a larger structure:

- Peter Coveney writes that "[t]he purpose and strength of . . ."
- We often say "Sorry" when we don't really mean it.
- And, instead of a comma, use a colon to set off explanatory or introductory language from a quoted element that is either very formal or long (especially if it's longer than one sentence):
- Peter Coveney had this to say about the nineteenth-century's use of children in fiction: "The purpose and strength of . . . . "

RULE #7
Use commas to set off phrases that express contrast.

- Some say the world will end in ice, not fire.
- It was her money, not her charm or personality, that first attracted him.
- The puppies were cute, but very messy.
- (Some writers will leave out the comma that sets off a contrasting phrase beginning with *but*.)

RULE # 8
Use a comma **to avoid confusion**. This is often a matter of consistently applying rule #3.

- For most the year is already finished.
- For most, the year is already finished.

- Outside the lawn was cluttered with hundreds of broken branches.

- Outside, the lawn was cluttered with hundreds of broken branches.

RULE # 9
Grammar English's Famous Rule of Punctuation: Never use only one comma between a subject and its verb. "Believing completely and positively in oneself is essential for success." [Although readers might pause after the word "oneself," there is no reason to put a comma there.]

RULE # 10
Typographical Reasons: Between a city and a state [Hartford, Connecticut], a date and the year [June 15, 1997], a name and a title when the title comes after the name [Bob Downey, Professor of English], in long numbers [5,456,783 and $14,682], etc. Although you will often see a comma between a name and suffix — Bob Downey, Jr., Richard Harrison, III — this comma is no longer regarded as necessary by most copy editors, and some individuals — such as Martin Luther King Jr. — never used a comma there at all.

Compounds, subject, sentence

15 Sentences Using Compound Subjects and Compound Verbs

Looking for sentences using compound subjects and compound verbs? Here are 15 sentences using compound subjects and 15 sentences using compound verbs along with a quick review of compound subjects and compound verbs.

Defining a Compound Subject

The subject of a sentence is generally defined as the noun or pronoun engaging in the activity of the verb. For example, study the following sentences:

- Beth reads very slowly.
- She reads very slowly.

In the first sentence, "Beth" is the subject. In the second sentence, "She" is the subject. In both sentences, the subject is engaged in the activity of reading.

When a sentence has two or more subjects, that's called a "compound subject." The individual subjects in a compound subject are joined by a **coordinating conjunction** (and, or, neither, nor). When the subjects are joined by "and," the verb agrees with the pronoun "they."

- Joanie and Chachi love each other. (NOT Joanie and Chachi loves each other.)

When the subjects are joined by "or" or "neither/nor," the verb agrees with the subject that is closest to the verb.

- The *piano* or the *book case* has to go.
- The *piano* or the *tables* have to go.
- Neither the *pillows* nor the *curtains* match the couch.
- Neither the *pillows* nor the *blanket* looks good in this room.

Defining a Compound Verb

A compound verb, or compound predicate, is used when the subject does more than one thing. You could write separate sentences for each verb, but if the subject is the same, that's just not necessary.

EXAMPLE:
- John paints beautifully. + John sells his work from time to time.
- = John *paints* beautifully and *sells* his work from time to time.

Compound verbs, like compound subjects, are also combined with a coordinating conjunction. The above example used "and," but you can also use other conjunctions.

- Mike either *lies* all the time or *has* the most extraordinary life I've ever seen.
- Alice neither *likes* the water nor *has* any plans to get in it.

COMPOUND SUBJECTS AND COMPOUND VERBS IN ACTION

Compound Subjects:

The following 15 sentences use compound subjects:

- *Potato chips* and *cupcakes* are bad for you.
- *Uncle Jim, Aunt Sue* and my cousin *Jake* went to Jamaica on vacation.
- *Beth* and *Kendra* read very slowly.

- The *boots* by the door and the *flip-flops* in the living room need to be put away.

- Neither the *boots* by the door nor the *flip-flops* in the living room will be here any more if you don't put them away.

- Neither a tall *man* nor a short *man* lives in that house.

- Neither *wind* nor *rain* nor *sleet* nor *hail* can stop the US Postal Service from delivering the mail.

- Neither the *rugs* downstairs nor the *carpet* upstairs has been vacuumed.

- Either *you* or your *brother* is going to be punished.

- Either the *chicken* or the *beef* in the freezer needs to be thawed for dinner tonight.

- Either the *matches* or the *candles* caused the fire.

- Either a *rat* or the *gerbil* keeps chewing up all my socks!

- *Everything on the bed* and *everything in the closet* was organized in under an hour.

- *Nobody in the bank* and *nobody in the store* saw the accident.

- *Anyone on the soccer team* and *anybody on the basketball team* is eligible for the scholarship.

Compound Verbs:

The following 15 sentences use compound verbs:

- The "victim" *sprayed* her assailant with pepper spray, *punched* him in the nose, kicked him in the groin, and ripped out his nipple ring.

- Last night, we *drank* a bottle of wine and *watched* a movie.

- Every Sunday, Sherri *goes* to the store and *buys* food for the week.

- My cats *lie* around all day and *run* around all night.

- Her husband *fixes* things that break around the house, *irons* better than she does, and *bakes* the best apple crisp you've ever tasted.

- I either *get* a lot done during the day or *do* nothing at all.

- The weekend either *flies* by or *drags* on forever, depending on what you're doing.

- The rain here either *mists* or *drenches*.

- Someone either *hit* my car with a shopping basket or *backed* into it as they were leaving.

- *Stay* or *go*; I don't *care* which.

- He neither *wants* nor *needs* to take a vacation.

- They neither *have* the money nor *want* to give it to him.

- Carol neither *likes* nor *dislikes* the wall color.

- She neither *eats* nor *drinks* nor *sleeps* nor *talks* to anyone since he left.
- We have neither *seen* each other nor *spoken* since our first date.

Conjuctions

What Are Conjunctions

Conjunctions are little words like and, but, and or. They're used to connect concepts, clauses, or parts of sentences.

- *I was going to see a movie, but I've changed my mind.*
- *She couldn't decide if she wanted the lemon tea or the rosehip tea.*

Uses for Conjunctions

Conjunctions connect thoughts, ideas, actions, nouns, clauses, etc.

- *Martha went to the market and bought fresh vegetables.*

In this sentence, the conjunction *and* connects the two things Martha did.

- *Martha went to the market, and I went to the hardware store.*

Here, *and* connects two sentences, preventing the choppiness which would arise if we used too many short sentences.

Conjunctions can also make lists.

- *I can't decide between the blue shirt and the red shirt.*
- *We barbequed hamburgers, hotdogs, and sausages.*

When using a conjunction, make sure that the parts which are being joined by the conjunction have a parallel structure (i.e. that they use the same verb forms, etc.)

- *I worked quickly yet am careful.*

Am careful is not in the same form as *quickly*; this creates faulty parallelism. The verbs need to be in the same form.

- *I worked quickly yet carefully.*

The two adverbs modify the verb *worked*.

- *I am quick yet careful.*

The two adjectives modify the pronoun *I*.

Context

Examples of Context Clues

A context clue is a source of information about a word that helps readers understand the word. This word or phrase offers insight, either directly or indirectly, into the word's meaning.

Synonyms as Context Clues
- It was an idyllic day; sunny, warm and perfect for a walk in the park.
- She hums continuously, or all the time, and it annoys me.

- The dates are listed in chronological order. They start at the beginning and end with the last event.

- Her animosity, or hatred, of her sister had divided the family.

- Bill felt remorse, or shame, for his harsh words.

- This situation is a conundrum - a puzzle.

Antonyms as Context Clues
- Emma had a lot of anxiety about the exam but I had no worries about it.

- Marty is gregarious, not like his brother who is quiet and shy.

- She is a famous singing star in her country but unknown to the rest of the world.

- I am willing to hike in the mountains, but he is reluctant because it gets so cold walking up and down the trails.

- Avoiding the accident was futile. Both cars did not have time to stop before crashing.

Definitions as Context Clues
- There is great prosperity in the country but many citizens are living in poverty.

- Some celestial bodies, such as the planets and stars, can be seen with the naked eye.

- The manager wanted a weekly inspection, which is a methodical examination of all the equipment.

- There was a lot of tangible evidence, including fingerprints and DNA, to prove them guilty.
- There is a 30 percent chance of precipitation, such as snow or sleet.

Explanations as Context Clues
- The team was elated when they won the trophy.
- During the demonstration, a skirmish broke out and the police were called to restore order.
- The cat has a kind disposition and would never bite or claw anyone.
- His constant questioning of my remarks made him a nuisance.
- Something in the refrigerator has a putrid odor; the smell was rotten when we opened the door.
- He winced in pain when he hit his thumb with the hammer.

Comparisons as Context Clues
- Diane was lethargic and didn't have the energy to get out of bed.
- The greatest trip I ever took was my expedition to Africa.
- Eating nutritious food is just as important as regular exercise.
- I am determined to graduate with honor and my friend is just as resolute.
- Sometimes he is perplexed by Sudoku puzzles, but others find them much easier to solve than a crossword puzzle.

Contrasts as Context Clues

- The picture of the landscape is picturesque but the one of the old house is ugly.

- The feral cat would not let us pet him, unlike our tame cat.

- Cold weather soon replaced the sweltering heat of summer.

- The hero was virtuous, not like the evil villain.

- The winner of the gold medal was omnipotent against his weaker opponents.

Contractions

About Contractions

Since the word contract means to squeeze together, it seems only logical that a contraction is two words made shorter by placing an apostrophe where letters have been omitted.

Examples of common contractions in the English language include:

- I'm: I am
- Can't: can not
- We've: we have
- She'll: she will
- He's: he is
- They'd: they would
- Won't: will not
- Weren't: were not
- Wasn't: was not
- Wouldn't: would not
- Shouldn't: should not
- Isn't: is not

Technically speaking, contractions aren't necessary in written English. Using the full version of a word is always grammatically correct. However, there are a number of reasons why contractions do serve a valuable stylistic purpose.

EXAMPLES:

- Contractions make your writing seem friendly and accessible. They give the appearance that you are actually "talking" to your reader.

- When writing dialogue in a novel or play, contractions help reflect how a character actually speaks.

- Contractions help to save space when preparing advertisements, slogans, and other written works that must be short and to the point.

It's and Its

It's and *its* are two of the most commonly confused words in the English language. However, understanding the difference between these two words is crucial for successful communication.

It's is a contraction for *it is* or *it has*.

EXAMPLES:

- I think it's going to snow on Monday.
- It's been a long time since I last saw Ben.
- It's a small world after all.

Its is a possessive pronoun. *Its* modifies a noun and is used to show ownership.

EXAMPLES:

- The bear carried its cub in its mouth.
- Nothing can take its place.
- The cat licked with its tongue.

To determine if you should use it's or *its* in your sentence, simply try replacing the word with *it is* or *it has*. If the sentence makes sense, it's is appropriate. If not, use *its*.

EXAMPLES:

- "Nothing can take it is place" makes no sense. Therefore, the correct word to use is *its*.
- "It is raining outside" is a perfectly acceptable sentence. Therefore, you may use *it's* if you wish.

They're, Their and There

They're, their and *there* are also quite commonly confused words among students who are learning about contractions.

They're is a contraction for *they are*.

EXAMPLES:

- They're happy to see me.
- I think they're very nice boys.
- In my opinion, they're a fine group of athletes.

Their is a possessive pronoun. It is used when you want to show that something belongs to someone.

EXAMPLES:
- Their new home is in San Diego.
- Their address is 517 West Maple.
- What is their phone number?

There is used to mean that something is at or in a particular place.

EXAMPLES:
- There is a present on the table.
- There are green beans on my plate, but I asked for broccoli.
- Look over there to see the ocean.

Deciding which word to use is easy if you remember a few simple tips:

- If you can replace the questionable word with *they are, they're* is correct.
- If you can replace the questionable word with *his* or *her, their* is correct.
- If you can replace the questionable word with *here, there* is correct.

Using Contractions in Formal Writing

While contractions can be very useful in written English, many experts caution against the use of contractions in formal communication. Since contractions tend to add a light and informal tone to your writing, they are often inappropriate for academic research papers, business presentations, and other types of official correspondence. However, this rule does have some flexibility. In general, it's best to use your own judgment when deciding if contractions are appropriate for a particular piece.

End of Sentence Contractions

Contractions can be used in any position in a sentence; however, homophone contractions such as "it's" and "they're" sound better when followed by another word or phrase. The reason is that the sounds of "its" and "it's" and "they're" and "they are" are so similar that they can be confusing unless they are used with the context of an additional word.

EXAMPLES:
- **Incorrect:** "It is what it's."
- **Correct:** "It is what it is looking like."
- **Correct:** "It is what it is."
- **Incorrect:** "You said they didn't want to go, well, they're."
- **Correct:** ""You said they didn't want to go, well, they're going."
- **Correct:** "You said they didn't want to go, well

Digraphs

A **digraph** is a single sound, or **phoneme**, which is represented by two letters. A **trigraph** is a phoneme which consists of three letters. However, many people will simply use the term 'digraph' generally to describe both combinations. In digraphs, consonants join together to form a kind of consonant team, which makes a special sound. For instance, *p* and *h* combine to form *ph*, which makes the /f/ sound as in *phonemic*.

When two or more consonants appear together and you hear each sound that each consonant would normally make, the consonant team is called a **consonant blend**. For instance, the word *blend* has two consonant blends: *bl*, for which you hear the sounds for both *b* and *l*, and *nd*, for which you hear the sounds for both *n* and *d*.

Digraph

- *ch*, which makes the /ch/ sound as in *watch*, *chick*, *chimpanzee*, and *champion*
- *ck*, which makes the /k/ sound as in *chick*
- *ff*, which makes the /f/ sound as in *cliff*
- *gh*, which makes the /g/ sound as in *ghost* and *ghastly*
- *gn*, which makes the /n/ sound as in *gnome* and *gnarled*
- *kn*, which makes the /n/ sound as in *knife* and *knight*
- *ll*, which makes the /l/ sound as in *wall*
- *mb*, which makes the /m/ sound as in *lamb* and *thumb*
- *ng*, which makes the /ng/ sound as in *fang*, *boomerang*, and *fingerprint*

- *nk*, which makes the /nk/ sound as in *ink*, *sink* and *rink*
- *ph*, which makes the /f/ sound as in *digraph*, *phone*, and *phonics*
- *qu*, which makes the /kw/ sound as in *quick*
- *sh*, which makes the /sh/ sound as in *shore*, *shipwreck*, *shark*, and *shield*
- *ss*, which makes the /s/ sound as in *floss*
- *th*, which makes the /th/ sound as in *athlete*, *toothbrush*, *bathtub*, *thin*, and *thunderstorm*
- *th*, which makes the /th/ sound as in *this*, *there*, and *that*
- *wh*, which makes the /hw/ sound as in *where* and *which*
- *wr*, which makes the /wr/ sound as in *write*
- *zz*, which makes the /z/ sound as in *fuzz* and *buzz*

Trigraphs
- *chr*, which makes the /chr/ sound as in *chrome* and *chromosome*
- *dge*, which makes the /g/ sound as in *dodge* and *partridge*
- *tch*, which makes the /tch/ sound as in *catch* and *match*

Footnotes & Bibliography

The Use of Footnotes

Footnotes are the acceptable method of acknowledging material which is not your own when you use it in an essay. Basically, footnoted material is of three types:

- Direct quotations from another author's work. (These must be placed in quotation marks).
- Citing authority for statements which are not quoted directly.
- Material of an explanatory nature which does not fit into the flow of the body of the text.

In the text of an essay, material to be footnoted should be marked with a raised number immediately *following* the words or ideas that are being cited.

EXAMPLE:
"The only aspect of Frontenac's conduct the king...did not condemn was his care for military security," Eccles stated, condemning Frontenac's administration.[2]

The footnotes may be numbered in sequence on each page or throughout the entire essay.

I. FORM AND CONTENT OF FOOTNOTES:

A. From a book:
[1]W. J. Eccles, *Frontenac The Courtier Governor* (Toronto: McClelland and Stewart Limited, 1959), 14.

[The information given in a footnote includes the author, the title, the place of publication, the publisher, the date of publication and the page or pages on which the quotation or information is found.]

B. From an article in a journal:
[1]Peter Blickle, "Peasant Revolts in the German Empire in the Late Middle Ages," *Social History,* Vol. IV, No. 2 (May, 1979), 233.

C. From a book containing quotations from other sources:
[1]Eugene A. Forsey, "Was the Governor General's Refusal Constitutional?", cited in Paul Fox, *Politics: Canada* (Toronto: McGraw-Hill Company of Canada Ltd., 1966), 186.

D. From a standard reference work:
[1]Norman Ward, "Saskatchewan," in *The Canadian Encyclopedia,* 2nd ed., Vol. 3, 1935.

[2]J. K. Johnson and P. B. Waite, "Macdonald, Sir John Alexander," in *The Dictionary of Canadian Biography,* Vol. 12, 599

E. From the Internet:
In citing material read on the Internet, it is not sufficient to indicate the website alone. You must provide information about author, title, and date of the document you are using, as follows:

[1]T. J. Pritzker, (1993). "An Early Fragment from Central Nepal" [Online]. Available: http://www.ingress.com/~astanart/pritzker/pritzker.html [1995, June].

The final date [1995, June] is the date the website was consulted.

For more information about how to cite electronic information see Xia Li and Nancy Crane, *The Handbook for Citing Electronic Resources* or http://www.uvm.edu/~ncrane/estyles/.

II. RULES TO REMEMBER IN WRITING FOOTNOTES:

- Titles of books, journals or magazines should be underlined or italicized.
- Titles of articles or chapters—items which are only a part of a book--are put in quotation marks.

III. ABBREVIATING IN FOOTNOTES:

The *first* time any book or article is mentioned in a footnote, all the information requested above must be provided. After that, however, there are shortcuts which should be used:

A. Several quotations in sequence from the same book:

The abbreviation to be used is "Ibid.," a Latin word meaning "in the same place." (Notice that Ibid. is not underlined). Ibid. can be used by itself, if you are referring to the same page as the previous footnote does, or it can be combined with a page number or numbers.

EXAMPLE:

¹Gerald Friesen, *The Canadian Prairies: A History* (Toronto: University of Toronto Press, 1984), 78.

²Ibid.

³Ibid., 351.

B. Reference to a source that already has been cited in full form but not in the reference *immediately preceding,* is made by using the author's last name (but not the first name or initials unless another author of the same surname has been cited), the title--in shortened form, if desired--and the page number.

EXAMPLE:

¹William Kilbourn, *The Firebrand* (Toronto: Clark, Irwin and Company Limited, 1956), 35.

²John L. Tobias, "Canada's Subjugation of the Plains Cree, 1879-1885," in *Sweet Promises: A Reader on Indian-White Relations in Canada,* ed. J. R. Miller (Toronto: University of Toronto Press, 1991), 224.

³Kilbourn, *The Firebrand,* 87.

⁴Tobias, "Canada's Subjugation of the Plains Cree," 22

Bibliography

The bibliography should be on a separate page. It should list the relevant sources used in the research for the paper. This list should be arranged alphabetically by the surname of the author. (Unlike the footnote reference, the surname is shown first, set off from the rest of the information.) The information required is: author, title, place of publication, publisher and date of publication.

NOTE: The information is separated for the most part by periods (rather than by commas, as in the footnotes) and the parentheses enclosing the facts of publication are dropped.

EXAMPLE:

Eccles, W. J. *Frontenac The Courtier Governor.* Toronto: McClelland and Stewart Limited, 1959.

Johnson, J. K. and P. B. Waite. "Macdonald, Sir John Alexander." In *The Dictionary of Canadian Biography,* Vol. 12, 591-612.

Koenigsberger, H. G. and George L. Mosse. *Europe in the Sixteenth Century.* London: Longmans, 1971.

Laslett, Peter. "The Gentry of Kent in 1640," *Cambridge Historical Journal,* Vol. IX, No. 2 (Spring 1948): 18-35.

Pritzker, T. J. (1993). "An Early Fragment from Central Nepal," [Online]. http://www.ingress. com/~astanart/pritzker   /pritzker.html. [1995 June].

Tobias, John L. "Canada's Subjugation of the Plains Cree, 1879-1885." In *Sweet Promises: A Reader on Indian-White Relations in Canada,* ed. J. R. Miller. Toronto: University of Toronto Press, 1991: 212-240.

Ward, N. "Saskatchewan." In *The Canadian Encyclopedia,* 2nd ed., Vol. 3, 1931-1938.

Homophones, Homonym and Homographs

They perplex us, confuse us, and make our heads spin. If you thought learning how to correctly spell words that sound alike was difficult, wait till you try to learn the terms for describing those words.

Homophones

Homophones are words that are pronounced alike but have different meanings.

Some examples are *accept* and *except*, *affect* and *effect*, and triplets *too* and *to* and *two*, along with *they're* and *their* and *there*.

Homophones may also refer to words that are spelled and pronounced the same, but differ in meaning, for example *lie* (lie down) and *lie* (an untruth).

These words are a major source of frustration for many writers, students, and professionals who struggle to memorize variant spellings for words that sound alike but have different meanings. English teachers and other spelling perfectionists wince when homophones are written incorrectly.

Worst of all, spell check won't catch the error when incorrect homophones are used because alternative spellings are legitimate.

Homonyms

And to confuse matters further, there are other words called homonyms, which are spelled and pronounced alike but have different meanings. Examples include words like stalk, which could refer to the stem of a plant (a stalk of corn), or the act pursuing or approaching prey (the cat stalked the mouse).

Another example of a homonym is *lie* — as in lie down or telling a *lie* (or untruth).

That's right, some homophones can also be classified as homonyms – if they're spelled the same. Confused yet? Wait. There's more.

Homographs

Homographs are words that are spelled the same but have different meanings. They may be pronounced the same or they could be pronounced differently from one another.

This means that some homographs are homophones and homonyms.

A good homograph example is *record* (a disc that plays audio) and *record* (to save or register something – in writing, audio, video, etc.).

How To Remember Homophones, Homonyms, and Homographs

It's not easy but it can be done. You can remember the difference (what difference there is) between homophones, homonyms, and homographs by breaking each word down and recalling the meaning of its root suffix and prefix. Also, try remembering each term separately to start, and don't worry about which homophones are homonyms and which homonyms are homographs.

The root *homo* means "the same." For all of these words something is the same – the spelling or the pronunciation.

- Homophones sound alike. That's the only rule and you can remember by the suffix *phone*, a word you can surely relate to sound. They may be spelled alike or not but they must sound alike.

- Homonyms are spelled alike. Same name. Name = nym. Like the words "same" and "name" they also sound alike.

- Homographs look alike (same spelling). Like graphs, they are visual. With the prefix *homo*, they are visually the same.

Nouns

Types of Nouns

There are several ways to classify the types of nouns that exist in the English language. In traditional grammar, nouns are taught to be words that refer to people, places, things, or abstract ideas. While modern linguistics find this definition to be problematic because it relies on non-specific nouns such as thing to specifically define what a noun is, much of our social understanding of what nouns are defers to the traditional definition.

Classifications of Nouns

Proper Nouns

Proper nouns are nouns that refer to specific entities. Writers of English capitalize proper nouns like *Nebraska, Steve, Harvard,* or *White House* to show their distinction from common nouns.

Common Nouns

Common nouns refer to general, unspecific categories of entities. Whereas *Nebraska* is a proper noun because it signifies a specific state, the word *state* itself is a common noun because it can refer to any of the 50 states in the United States. *Harvard* refers to a particular institution of higher learning, while the common noun *university* can refer to any such institution.

Countable Nouns

To linguists, these count nouns can occur in both single and plural forms, can be modified by numerals, and can co-occur with quantificational determiners like *many, most, more, several,* etc.

For example, the noun *bike* is a countable noun. Consider the following sentence:

- There is a *bike* in that garage.

In this example, the word *bike* is singular as it refers to one bike that is presently residing in a particular garage.

However, *bike* can also occur in the plural form.

- There are *six broken bikes* in that garage.

In this example, the noun *bikes* refers to more than one bike as it is being modified by the numeral *six*.

In addition, countable nouns can co-occur with quantificational determiners.

- In that garage, *several bikes* are broken.

This sentence is grammatical, as the noun *bike* can take the modification of the quantificational determiner *several*.

Uncountable Nouns or Mass Nouns

Conversely, some nouns are not countable and are called uncountable nouns or mass nouns. For example, the word *clutter* is a mass noun.

- That garage is full of *clutter*.

This sentence makes grammatical sense. However, the following example does not.

- That garage is full of *clutters*.

Mass nouns can not take plural forms, and therefore a sentence containing the word *clutters* is ungrammatical.

Substances, liquids, and powders are entities that are often signified by mass nouns such as *wood, sand, water,* and *flour*. Other examples would be *milk, air, furniture, freedom, rice,* and *intelligence*.

Collective Nouns

In general, collective nouns are nouns that refer to a group of something in a specific manner. Often, collective nouns are used to refer to groups of animals. Consider the following sentences.

- Look at the *gaggle* of geese.
- There used to be *herds* of wild buffalo on the prairie.
- A *bevy* of swans is swimming in the pond.
- A *colony* of ants live in the anthill.

In the above examples, *gaggle, herds, bevy,* and *colony* are collective nouns.

Concrete Nouns

Concrete nouns are nouns that can be touched, smelled, seen, felt, or tasted. *Steak, table, dog, Maria, salt,* and *wool* are all examples of concrete nouns.

- Can I pet your *dog*?
- Please pass the *salt*.
- Your sweater is made of fine *wool*.

Concrete nouns can be perceived by at least one of our senses.

Abstract Nouns

More ethereal, theoretical concepts use abstract nouns to refer to them. Concepts like *freedom, love, power,* and *redemption* are all examples of abstract nouns.

- They hate us for our *freedom*.
- All you need is *love*.
- We must fight the *power*.

In these sentences, the abstract nouns refer to concepts, ideas, philosophies, and other entities that cannot be concretely perceived.

Pronouns

Personal pronouns are types of nouns that take the place of nouns when referring to people, places or things. The personal pronouns in English are *I, you, he, she, it,* and *they.*

- Amy works at a flower shop.
  She works at a flower shop.
- The Greeks invented democracy.
  They invented democracy.

These pronouns take on other forms depending on what type of function they are performing in a sentence. For example, when used to signify possession of another noun, pronouns take on their possessive form such as *mine, ours, hers,* and *theirs.*

- That pizza belongs to Marley.
  That pizza is *hers.*

When used as the object of a preposition, pronouns take on their objective case. Examples include *him, her, me, us,* and *them.*

- Hand the money over to Jennifer.
  Hand the money over to *her.*

- The police are on to John and Ray.
  The police are on to *them*.

Bottom line: There are nine types or classifications of nouns, each designed to serve a different purpose in a sentence.

Outlining

Are there still rules to follow in making an Outline?

Definitely, there are set of rules that you need to consider if you are planning to make an effective outline. If you are to follow these rules you will reap the fruits of it. The purposes, Remember??

Here are the rules:

RULE 1.
Arrangement

An outline, whether sentence or topic, is divided into points and subpoints.

Subpoints always go under the main points of which they are a part and which they support.

EXAMPLE:

I. *Kinds of apples*
    A. *Jonathan*
    B. *Granny Smith*
    C. *Macintosh*

The divisions in any series should be of equal importance. That is, the heads numbered I, II, III, IV, etc., should be the main divisions of a paper; divisions lettered with capitals should be sub-divisions of heads and numbered with Roman numerals.

EXAMPLE:

Properly Divided:

I. The executive branch
    A. The President
    B. The Cabinet

II. The legislative branch
    A. The House
    B. The Senate

III. The judicial branch
    A. The Supreme Court
    B. The lower courts

Improperly Divided:

I. The executive branch
    II. The President
    III. The Cabinet

IV. The legislative branch
    V. The House
    VI. The Senate

VII. The judicial branch
    VIII. The Supreme Court
    IX. The lower courts

RULE 2.

Co-ordination

Points of equal importance should be coordinated - that is, given an equal and parallel ranking. It would be illogical to outline our national defenses thus:

I. The armed services
    A. The Army
    B. The Navy
    C. The Marines

II. The Air Force

The four divisions, being of equal importance, should be parallel:

I. The armed services
    A. The Army
    B. The Navy
    C. The Marines
    D. The Air Force

Parallel points in an outline should not overlap, as they do, for example, in the following:

I. American automobiles
II. Ford

The following would be better:

I. American automobiles
    A. Ford
    B. Chevrolet

II. Foreign automobiles

RULE 4.
Single sub-point

Do not use single sub-points in an outline. When you divide anything, you always have at least two parts. Thus, if you have an *A.*, you should have a *B.*; a *1.*

should be followed by a 2. If you think that you have only one subtopic, include it in the topic above.

EXAMPLE:
Instead of writing:

I. Large, sparsely populated states are hard for salesmen to cover.
    A. Montana is one of these states.

Write:

I. Large, sparsely populated states like Montana are hard for salesmen to cover.

RULE 5.
Parallelism

If *I.* is a pronoun, *II.* should be a pronoun; if *A.* under *I.* is an adjective, *B.* under *I.* should also be an adjective.

RULE 6.
Consistency

In a topic outline, all points and sub-points must be words, phrases, or clauses. In a sentence outline, all points must be sentences. In other words, do not mix topic and sentence outlines.

RULE 7.
Numbering and lettering

Periods, not dashes, should be placed after these figures and letters.

RULE 8.
Capitalization

Capitalize the first word of every point and subpoint and only such other words as would naturally be capitalized.

RULE 9.
Punctuation

Use a period after each number or letter indicating a point. Do not use a period at the end of a line unless the point or subpoint is a sentence.

RULE 10.
Indentation

Indent equally headings of the same rank. Corresponding letters or numbers - *I, II, III; A, B, C; 1, 2, 3* - should be kept in vertical columns. If a subtopic is too long for one line, the second line should line up under the first word of the line above. Do not write directly under the symbol when a line runs over; i.e., use hanging indents.

I. _____
   A. _____
   B. _____
      1. _____
         _____
      2. _____
         _____
         a. _____
         b. _____
            i. _____
            ii. _____
II. _____

Predicates

What Is the Predicate of a Sentence? (with Examples)
The predicate is the part of a sentence (or clause) which tells us what the subject does or is. To put it another way, the predicate is everything that is not the subject.

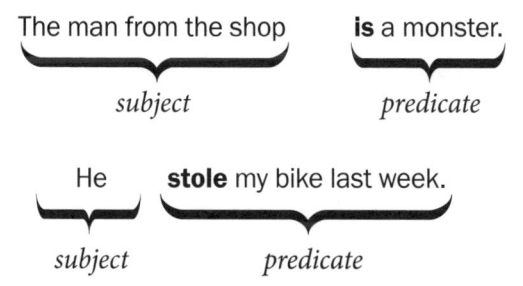

The man from the shop [*subject*] **is** a monster. [*predicate*]

He [*subject*] **stole** my bike last week. [*predicate*]

verb in bold

At the heart of the predicate is a verb. In addition to the verb, a predicate can contain direct objects, indirect objects, and various kinds of phrases.

A sentence has two parts; the subject and the predicate. The subject is what the sentence is about, and the predicate is a comment about the subject.

Examples of Predicates of Sentences
Here are some examples of predicates. In each example, the predicate of the sentence is italicized and the verb in the predicate is in bold.

- Elvis ***lives.***
- Adam ***lives** in Bangor.*
- The telegram ***contained** exciting news.*
- The girls in our office ***are** experienced instructors.*

- They **are** experienced instructors, who acquired their experience in France.

Predicates in Clauses

A clause contains a subject and predicate too. The examples below are all clauses not sentences. The predicate is italicized and the verb of the clause is in bold.

- who **lives** *with her mother*
  (The subject is the relative pronoun *who.*)

- which **was** *somewhat unexpected*
  (The subject is the relative pronoun *which.*)

- that **points** *to the North Pole*
  (The subject is the relative pronoun *that.*)

Predicates within Predicates

It is common for a clause to feature within a sentence predicate.

EXAMPLE:

- who **lives** *with our mother*

  (This is a clause. It is has its own subject and predicate.)

- Jane **is** *my youngest sister, who lives with our mother.*

  (Notice how the clause *who lives with our mother* (which has its own subject and predicate) is part of the longer sentence predicate.)

Predicate in a Sentence Starting There

When a sentence starts "There" + [verb to be], the word *there* is the not the subject. It is part of the predicate. Look at this example:

- There **is** a guy who works down our chip shop who swears he's Elvis.

    The subject is *a guy who works down our chip shop who swears he's Elvis.* Everything else is the predicate.

It helps if you write it like this:

- A guy who works down our chip shop who swears he's Elvis **is** *there*.

In structure, it is no different from this:

- He **is** *here*.

Prefix

Attaching Prefixes and Suffixes: Bits and Pieces

Prefixes are word parts you add to the beginning of a word to change its meaning; *suffixes* are word parts you add to the end of a word to change its meaning. Because many useful words are created by adding prefixes and suffixes to *root words*, you can save a lot of time wondering "Did I spell this sucker correctly?" by knowing how to add prefixes and suffixes. Let's take a look at the guidelines.

Attaching Prefixes: Front-End Collision

The rule here is simple: Don't add or omit a letter when you attach a prefix. Keep all the letters—every one of them. Here are some examples.

Prefix		Word		New Word
dis	+	satisfied	=	dissatisfied
mis	+	spell	=	misspell
un	+	acceptable	=	unacceptable
re	+	election	=	reelection
inter	+	related	=	interrelated

You Could Look It Up

Prefixes are word parts you add to the beginning of a word to change its meaning; suffixes are word parts you add to the end of a word to change its meaning.

Attaching Suffixes: Rear-End Collision

Keep all the letters when you add a suffix ... unless the word ends in a y or a silent e. We'll talk about *them* later. The following chart and guidelines show you how to master the suffix situation.

Word		Suffix		New Word
accidental	+	ly	=	accidentally
drunken	+	ness	=	drunkenness
ski	+	ing	=	skiing
foresee	+	able	=	foreseeable

Prepositions

Prepositions are relationship words. They give clues and guidance regarding how the remainder of the sentence fits together. There are several important rules when using prepositions in the context of a sentence. These rules relate to how prepositions can be used, which prepositions can be used when, and where prepositions have to go in the sentence.

What is a Preposition?

A preposition is a word that explains the time, space or logical relationship between the other parts of the sentence. In other words, it links all the other words together, so the reader can understand how the pieces of the sentence fit. There are hundreds of prepositions in the English language. One easy way to remember prepositions is that they are words that tell you everywhere a bunny can run.

EXAMPLE:
a bunny can run

- up
- down
- near
- far
- by
- at
- around
- close
- always

All of these words, and many more, are repositions.

Preposition Rules

There are 2 major rules when it comes to the use of prepositions.

- The first major rule deals with preposition choice. Certain prepositions must follow certain words, and the correct preposition must be used to make relationships between words in the sentences clear.

- The second major rule deals with the prepositions place in the sentence. Prepositions must be followed by nouns, and prepositions can only go on the end of the sentence in certain situations.

Preposition Choice

Determining the correct preposition to use can be a tricky proposition. This can be especially difficult when dealing with idioms- expressions in the English language that require the use of a certain word, simply because that is the word we have chosen to use. Idiomatic expressions are expressions you just have to memorize, and when errors are made, they are almost always preposition errors.

Here are some examples of idioms, along with the correct prepositions:

- Able *to*
- Capable *of*
- Preoccupied *with*
- Concerned *by*
- Prohibited *from*

Each of the italicized words are the only acceptable prepositions to follow these words. It would not be grammatically correct to say "able *with*" or "capable *to*"

Prepositions In the Context of Sentences

Prepositions must always be followed by a noun or pronoun. That noun is called the object of the preposition. A verb can't be the *object* of a preposition.

- The bone was *for* the dog.

  This is correct- the preposition *for* is followed by the noun "dog."

- The bone was for walked.

  This is not correct. The preposition *for* is followed by a verb "walked." Walked can't be the object of a preposition.

This rule may seem confusing at first, because you may have seen words that look like verbs following the preposition *to* in sentences.

EXAMPLE:
- I like *to ski*
- These boots are for *skiing.*

However, in these examples, the *ski* and *skiing* are not actually acting as verbs.

In the first example, *to ski* is part of the infinitive. An infinitive is NOT a verb. An infinitive occurs when a verb is used as a noun, adjective, or adverb. Here, "to ski" is a THING that the person likes doing, not an action that they are doing. It is a verbal noun.

In the second example, *skiing* is a gerund. Like an infinitive, a gerund is NOT a verb, but is instead a noun, adjective or adverb. Here, "skiing" is a thing that the boots are for. No one in this sentence is doing the action of skiing.

Using Prepositions at the End of Sentences

Because prepositions must be followed by a noun and have an object, they usually shouldn't be used at the end of a sentence. For example, it is not correct to say:

- The table is where I put my books on.

However, there are certain circumstances where it is acceptable to end a sentence with a preposition. These exceptions exist where the preposition is not extraneous. In other words, the preposition needs to be there, and if it wasn't, the meaning of the sentence would change.

In the above example, *"The table is where I put my books on."* the use of the preposition "on" isn't necessary. We could take the "on" out of the sentence and the meaning would be the same. So, the use of the preposition was extraneous or unnecessary and we don't need it.

However, here is an example where it is perfectly acceptable to use a preposition to end a sentence:

- "I turned the TV on."

Punctuation

Correct punctuation is essential for clear and effective writing. The following list contains some of the most critical punctuation rules.

Commas

Commas are used to separate parts of a sentence. They tell readers to pause between words or groups of words, and they help clarify the meanings of sentences.

- Commas are used to separate three or more words, phrases, or clauses in a series.

EXAMPLE:
Practice will be held before school, in the afternoon, and at night.

- Commas are used after an introductory dependent clause (a group of words before the subject of a sentence that do not form a complete sentence).

EXAMPLE:
If your friends enjoy Chinese food, they will love this restaurant.

- Commas are used to set off introductory words, introductory adverbial, participial, or infinitive phrases, and longer introductory prepositional phrases.

EXAMPLE:
Incidentally, I was not late this morning. (word)

Hoping for a bigger fish, Rob spent three more hours fishing. (phrase)

- Commas are used between independent clauses joined by a coordinating conjunction (for, and, nor, but, or, yet, so).

EXAMPLE:
My dog had fleas, so we gave him a bath.

- Commas set off nonessential phrases or clauses.

EXAMPLE:
The man, I think, had a funny laugh.

- Commas set off an appositive (a word or phrase that renames a noun).

EXAMPLE:
Tanya, Debbie's sister, gave a brilliant speech last night.

End of Sentence Punctuation

End of sentence punctuation is used to let the reader know when a thought is finished.

- A statement (or declarative sentence) is followed by a period.

EXAMPLE:
Orem is the home of Utah Valley State College.

- A direct question (or interrogative sentence) is followed by a question mark.

EXAMPLE:
When did Joe buy a red shirt?

- Do not use a question mark after a declarative sentence that contains an indirect question

EXAMPLE:
Marie wants to know when Joe bought a red shirt.

- An exclamatory sentence is followed by an exclamation point.

EXAMPLE:
What a good movie!

- Use exclamation marks sparingly because they can unnecessarily exaggerate sentences.

EXAMPLE:
Monet was the most influential painter of his time!
(Most emphasizes influential painter; therefore, an exclamation point is not needed.)

Semicolons
Semicolons are used to separate clauses or phrases that are related and that receive equal emphasis.

- Semicolons join independent clauses in a compound sentence if no coordinating conjunction is used.

EXAMPLE:
Michael seemed preoccupied; he answered our questions abruptly.

- Semicolons are used before a conjunctive adverb (transition word) that joins the clauses of a compound sentence.

EXAMPLE:
The emergency room was crowded; however, Warren was helped immediately.

- Semicolons help avoid confusion in lists where there are already commas.

EXAMPLE:
We traveled to London, England; Paris, France; Berlin, Germany; and Sofia, Bulgaria.

Colons

Colons follow independent clauses and are used to call attention to the information that comes after.

- Colons come after the independent clause and before the word, phrase, sentence, quotation, or list it is introducing.

EXAMPLE:
Joe has only one thing on his mind: girls. (word)

Joe has only one thing on his mind: the girl next door. (phrase)

Joe has only one thing on his mind: he wants to go out with Linda. (clause)

Joe has several things on his mind: his finals, his job, and Linda. (list)

- Never use a colon after a verb that directly introduces a list.

  INCORRECT:
  The things on Joe's mind are: finals, work, and Linda.

  CORRECT:
  The things on Joe's mind are finals, work, and Linda.

Hyphens

Hyphens are used to form compound words or join word units. They are used to join prefixes, suffixes, and letters to words.

- Use hyphens with compound numbers from twenty-one to ninety-nine and with fractions used as modifiers.

EXAMPLE:
forty-two applicants

two-thirds majority (*two-thirds* is an adjective modifying *majority*)

three-fourths empty (*three-fourths* is an adverb modifying *empty*)

two thirds of the voters (*two thirds* is not being used as an adjective here because *thirds* is a noun being modified by *two*)

- Hyphens in a compound adjective only when it comes before the word it modifies. However, some compound adjectives are always hyphenated, such as *well-balanced*. Look up compound adjectives in the dictionary if you are unsure whether or not to hyphenate them.

EXAMPLE:
a *well-liked* author an author who is *well liked*

a *world-renowned* composer a composer who is *world renowned*

- Use a hyphen with the prefixes ex-, self-, and all-; with the suffix -elect; and with all prefixes before a proper noun or proper adjective.

EXAMPLE:
all-star, ex-mayor, pro-Canadian, senator-elect, anti-Semitic, non-European, self-control, self-image

Dashes
Dashes connect groups of words to other groups of words in order to emphasize a point or show that the information is unessential. Usually the dash separates words in the middle of a sentence from the rest of the sentence, or it leads to material at the end of the sentence.

In the middle of a sentence, a dash can put special emphasis on a group of words or make them stand out from the rest of the sentence.

EXAMPLE:
BECOMES:
Linda Simpson's prescription for the economy, lower interest rates, higher employment, and less government spending, was rejected by the president's administration.

Linda Simpson's prescription for the economy—lower interest rates, higher employment, and less government spending—was rejected by the president's administration.

The dash can also be used to attach material to the end of a sentence when there is a clear break in the continuity of the sentence or when an explanation is being introduced.

EXAMPLE:
The president will be unable to win enough votes for another term of office—unless, of course, he can reduce unemployment and the deficit soon.

EXAMPLE:
It was a close call—the sudden gust of wind pushed the helicopter to within inches of the power line.

Apostrophes
Apostrophes are used to show possession or to indicate where a letter has been omitted to form a contraction.

- Show possession, add an apostrophe and an -s to singular nouns or indefinite pronouns that end in *one* or *body*.

EXAMPLE:
Susan's wrench, anyone's problem

- Add only an apostrophe for plural possessive nouns ending in -s.

EXAMPLE:
my parents' car, the musicians' instruments'

- Add an apostrophe and an -s for plural possessive nouns that do not end in -s.

EXAMPLE:
the men's department, my children's toys

- Add an apostrophe and an -s for singular possessive nouns that end in -s.

EXAMPLE:
Chris's cookbook, the business's system

Do not use an apostrophe with possessive personal pronouns including *yours, his, hers, its, ours, their,* and *whose.*

Apostrophes are also used in contractions, two words which have been combined into one, to mark where the missing letter or letters would be.

EXAMPLE:
I am = I'm
who is = who's
cannot = can't
you are = you're
I have = I've
let us = let's
he is, she is, it is = he's, she's, it's
they are = they're

Confusing *it's* with *its*.
It's is a contraction for *it is; its* is a possessive pronoun.

Quotation Marks
Quotation marks are used to show the beginning and end of a quotation or a title of a short work.

- Quotation marks enclose the exact words of a person (direct quotation).

EXAMPLE:
Megan said, *"Kurt has a red hat."*

- Do not use quotation marks around a paraphrase (using your own words to express the author's ideas) or a summary of the author's words.

EXAMPLE:
Megan said that Kurt's hat was red.

- Quotation marks set off the titles of magazine articles, poems, reports, and chapters within a book. (Titles of books, magazines, plays, and other whole publications should be underlined or italicized.)

EXAMPLE:
"The Talk of the Town" is a regular feature in Time magazine.

Quotation Marks with Other Punctuation
- Place periods and commas inside quotation marks.

EXAMPLE:
Aida said, *"Aaron has a blue shirt."*

- Place semicolons and colons outside quotation marks.

EXAMPLE:
He calls me his *"teddy bear"*; I'm not a bear.

- Place question marks or exclamation points inside the quotation marks if they punctuate the quotation only .

EXAMPLE:
"Are we too late?" she asked.

- Place question marks or exclamation points outside the quotation marks if they punctuate the entire sentence.

EXAMPLE:
Why did she say, *"We are too late"*?

Parentheses
Elements inside parentheses are related to the sentence but are nonessential.

- Parentheses set off additions or expressions that are not necessary to the sentence. They tend to de-emphasize what they set off.

EXAMPLE:
We visited several European countries (England, France, Spain) on our trip last year.

- Parentheses enclose figures within a sentence.

EXAMPLE:
Grades will be based on (1) participation, (2) in-class writing, and (3) exams.

- When the group inside the parentheses forms a complete sentence but is inserted inside a larger sentence, no period is needed. However, if a question mark or exclamation point is needed, it may be used.

EXAMPLE:
The snow (she saw it as she passed the window) was now falling heavily.

- When parentheses are used to enclose an independent sentence, the end punctuation belongs inside the parentheses.

EXAMPLE:
Mandy told me she saw Amy's new car. (I saw Amy's car before Mandy.) She said it was a nice car.

Sentences

The most common sentence problems in student writing are: comma splice and fused (or run-on) sentence, sentence fragment (or incomplete sentence), agreement, and shifts. If you are unfamiliar with these terms and others such as subject, verb, object, complement, phrase, main clause, independent clause, subordinate clause, coordinating conjunction, number, person, etc., you are strongly encouraged to research their meanings and application in a standard English grammar book.

Keep a few simple principles in mind:

Comma Splice And Fused (Or Run-On) Sentence

Do not link two main (independent) clauses with only a comma (comma splice) or run two main clauses together without any punctuation (fused sentence).

EXAMPLES:
Comma Splice:
The wind was cold, they decided not to walk.

Fused Sentence:
The wind was cold they decided not to walk.

To correct comma splices and fused sentences: 1) Place a period after the first main (independent) clause and write the second main clause as a sentence; 2) use a semi-colon to separate main clauses; or 3) insert a coordinating conjunction (and, but, or, for, nor, so, yet) after the comma; or 4) make one clause subordinate to the other.

REVISIONS:
The wind was cold. They decided not to walk.
The wind was cold; they decided not to walk.
The wind was cold, so they decided not to walk.
The wind was so cold that they decided not to walk.

Sentence Fragment

Avoid sentence fragments. The term fragment refers to a group of words beginning with a capital letter and ending with a period. Although written as if it were a sentence, a fragment is only a part of a sentence – such as a phrase or a subordinate clause.

EXAMPLES:
Larry always working in his yard on Saturdays.
Because he enjoys his flowers and shrubs.
Which help to screen his house from the street.
For example, a tall hedge with a border of petunias.

Eliminate fragments by making them into complete sentences or by connecting them to existing sentences. One way to eliminate many sentence fragments is to be sure that each word group has at least one subject and one predicate.

CORRECTIONS:
Larry always works in his yard on Saturdays. He enjoys the flowers and shrubs.

OR:

He enjoys the flowers and shrubs that help to screen his house from the street – for example, a tall hedge with a border of petunias.

Agreement

Make a verb agree in number with its subject; make a pronoun agree in number with its antecedent.

A singular subject takes a singular verb, and a plural subject takes a plural verb.

Singular:
The *car* in the lot *looks* shabby. [*car, looks*]

Plural:
The *cars* in the lot *look* shabby. [*cars, look*]

When a pronoun has an antecedent (an antecedent is the noun to which the pronoun refers), the noun and pronoun should agree in number.

Singular:
A dolphin has its own language. [*dolphin, its*]

Plural:
Dolphins have their own language. [*dolphins, their*]

Shifts
Avoid needless shifts in person and number.

Shift:
If a *person* is going to improve, *you* should work harder. [shift from third person to second person]

Better:
If *you* are going to improve, *you* should work harder. [second person]
OR
If *people* are going to improve, *they* should work harder. [third person]
OR
If *we* are going to improve, *we* should work harder. [first person]

Gender Referents

Avoid awkward "his/her" and "he/she" gender constructions.

Awkward:
The client is usually the best judge of his or her counseling.

Better:
The client is usually the best judge of the value of counseling. [Omit gender referents.]
OR
Clients are usually the best judges of the value of the counseling they receive. [Change to plural]
OR
The best judge of the value of counseling is usually the client. [Rephrase the sentence.]

Simile & Metaphors

Simile and Metaphor Examples

The simile and metaphor examples in this article take the form of four "rules" you should apply whenever you add similes and metaphors to your novel.

These two figures of speech are an important part of your writer's toolkit, but you should always beware of using them badly or too much.

Most of the examples of metaphors and similes given below are *bad* examples. If you want your novel to rise above the ordinary, avoid this kind of writing at all costs

Four Rules for Using Similes and Metaphors

RULE 1.
With Figures of Speech, Less Is Definitely More

Similes and metaphors are like the finishes touches in a room - a cranberry scatter cushion here, a Ming vase there, two Georgian candlesticks on the mantelpiece.

Used well, they beautify a passage of prose in a novel. Used too often, they make it look gaudy.

Solution? If in doubt, strike them out.

RULE 2.
Avoid the Commonplace

Take a look at these simile and metaphor examples.

- He drank like a fish
- She had the heart of a lion
- The town was as dead as a dodo
- She was mutton dressed as lamb
- He had skin like leather

What's wrong with them? Well, the first time these figures of speech were ever used, way back when, they would have been fresh and clever. Now they are not.

Find original and interesting figures of speech and publishers will sit up and take notice. Resort to similes and metaphors that come easily to mind and publishers, dare I say it, will avoid you like the plague.

(Yes, that final simile is definitely overused and one to avoid in your own writing.)

RULE 3.
Don't Use Two Similes Together

Using too many similes in general is not to be recommended, but using one right after the other is a definite no-no. It never looks right, as these simile examples show.

- She had skin like cream, hair like silk, and eyes like green marbles.
- He was as fearless as a lion and as fast as a cheetah.

- Frank stood on the edge of the diving board like a prisoner on the gallows. The short drop to the pool looked as daunting as the Grand Canyon.

RULE 4.
Don't Mix Metaphors

This is virtually the same point as the previous one, although the problem is a subtler one. Take a look at these two examples of metaphors.

- *Norman's mind was a machine. He could waltz through cryptic crosswords in mere minutes.*

The trouble here is that the message is confused. First, Norman's intelligence is compared to a clever and efficient machine. Next, his speed at crosswords is compared to the speed and grace of a dance.

If you don't want the reader to say "Huh?" you must always follow metaphors through once you have introduced them.

- *Norman's mind was a machine. He could process cryptic crosswords in mere minutes.*

Subject

Recognize a subject of a sentence when you see one.

In a **sentence,** every **verb** must have a subject. If the verb expresses action—like *sneeze, jump, bark,* or *study*—the subject is who or what does the verb.

Take a look at this example:

- During his biology lab, *Tommy* danced on the table.

Danced is an **action verb**. *Tommy* is who did the dancing. Look at the next example:

- The speeding *hotrod* crashed into a telephone pole.

Crashed is the action verb. The *hotrod* is what did the crashing.

Not all verbs are action verbs. Some verbs are linking: *am, is, are, was, were, seem,* and *become,* among others. **Linking verbs** connect the subject to something that is said about the subject. Take a look at this example:

- Ron's *bathroom* is a disaster.

Bathroom is the subject. *Is* connects the subject to something that is said about it, that the bathroom is a disaster. Here is another example:

- The bathroom *tiles* are fuzzy with mold.

The word *tiles* is the subject. *Are* connects *tiles* to something said about them, that they are fuzzy with mold.

Generally, but not always, the subject of a linking verb will come *before* the linking verb.

Know the difference between a *complete* subject and a *simple* subject.

The complete subject is *who* or *what* is doing the verb *plus* all of the **modifiers** [descriptive words] that go with it. Read the sentence below:

- The big, hungry, green Martian grabbed a student from the back row.

Who did the grabbing? The Martian, of course. But this Martian wasn't petite, satisfied, and blue. No, this one was big, hungry, and green. The complete subject, then, is *the huge, hairy, hungry, green Martian.*

The simple subject, on the other hand, is the *who* or *what* that is doing the verb *without* any description. Take a look at this example:

- The bright copper coin sparkled on the sidewalk.

What did the sparkling? Obviously, the bright copper coin. *The, bright* and *copper,* however, are just description that distinguishes this coin from one that is, let's say, tarnished and silver. The simple subject is only the word *coin.*

Remember that the subject is never part of a prepositional phrase.

The subject of a verb will never be part of a **prepositional phrase**. A prepositional phrase begins with a **preposition** [*in, on, at, between, among,* etc.] and ends with a **noun, pronoun,** or **gerund**. Look at these examples of prepositional phrases:

- in the dirty bathtub
- on the bumpy road
- at home
- between us
- among the empty pizza boxes
- without crying

Sometimes a prepositional phrase appears to be either the subject itself or part of the subject. Read the example that follows:

- Neither of these boys wants to try a piece of pineapple pizza.

In this sentence, the *boys* seem to be the ones who do not want the pizza, but because they are part of a prepositional phrase, *of these boys*, they are not the subject. *Neither* is the actual subject. Take a look at another example:

- My dog, along with her seven puppies, has chewed all of the stuffing out of the sofa cushions.

Here, both *my dog* and *her seven puppies* are chewing on the sofa, but because the puppies are part of the prepositional phrase *along with her seven puppies*, the only word that counts as the subject is *dog*.

Remember this additional point:

Generally, but not always, the subject comes before the verb, as in all of the examples above. There are, however, exceptions, like this one:

- In a small house adjacent to our backyard lives a *family* with ten noisy children.

Lives is the **action verb** in this sentence, but it is not the house or the backyard that is doing the living. Instead, it is the family with ten noisy children. *Family*, then, is the subject of this sentence, even though it comes after the verb. Take a look at another example:

- Around the peach trees are several buzzing *bumblebees*.

Are is the **linking verb** in this sentence. The word *trees*, however, is not the subject because *trees* is within the prepositional phrase *around the peach trees*. The subject in this sentence, *bumblebees*, follows the verb rather than coming before it.

Subject-Verb Agreement

Subject verb agreement simply means the subject and verb must agree in number. This means both need to be singular or both need to be plural.

Subject/Verb Agreement Examples

Here are some examples of subject verb agreement (the subject is bolded and the verb italicized):

- My **dog** always *growls* at the postal carrier.
- **Basketballs** *roll* across the floor.
- **I** don't *understand* the assignment.
- These **clothes** *are* too small for me.
- **Peter** doesn't *like* vegetables.

Compound Subjects

Compound subjects (two subjects in the same sentence) usually take a plural verb, unless the combination is treated as singular in popular usage or the two subjects refer to the same thing or person. Here are some examples of subject verb agreement with compound subjects:

- **Sugar and flour** *are* needed for the recipe.
- **Neither my dad nor my brothers** *know* how to ski.
- **Pepperoni and cheese** *are* great on a pizza.
- **Corned beef and cabbage** *is* a traditional meal in Ireland. (popular usage)
- **The creator and producer** *is* arriving soon. (both refer to same person)

When using "or" or "nor" in a compound subject containing a singular and plural subject, the verb agrees with the closest subject. Examples of compound subjects using or, neither-nor, or either-or include:

- **My mom or dad** *is* coming to the play. (singular)
- **Neither gray nor white** *is* my favorite color. (singular)
- Either **Grandpa or my sisters** *are* going to the park. (closest subject is plural)
- Either **my sisters or Grandpa** *is* going to the park. (closest subject is singular)
- Neither **she nor I** *am* going to college. (closest subject is singular)

Singular Indefinite Pronouns

Here are some examples of subject verb agreement with singular indefinite pronouns:

- **Each** *gets* a trophy for playing.
- **Somebody** *will pay* for this.
- **Anybody** *is* more fun than you.
- **Something** *is* very wrong here.
- **Everybody** *enjoys* a good book.
- **Nothing** *has* been determined as of yet.

Plural Indefinite Pronouns

Here are some examples of subject verb agreement with plural indefinite pronouns:

- **Both** *are* qualified for the job.
- **Many** *went* to the beach and got sunburned.
- **Few** *know* what it really takes to get ahead.
- **Several** *are* already on location.
- **Some** sugar *is* required for taste. (sugar is uncountable so singular verb used)
- **Most** of the cookies *were* eaten. (cookies are countable so plural verb used)

Midsentence Phrase or Clause

Here are some examples of subject verb agreement with a phrase or clause between the subject and verb:

- A **theory** of physics *ascertains* that a body in motion stays in motion.
- A **virus** in all the company's computers *is* a real threat to security.
- The **causes** of this prevalent disease *are* bad diet and lack of exercise.
- The **couch and chair** I got at the store *look* really nice in here.
- The **members** of the choir *are* very happy with the performance.

Collective Nouns

Collective nouns can be singular or plural depending on meaning. Here are some examples of subject verb agreement with collective nouns:

- The **committee** *meets* here every Thursday. (singular)
- The **crowd** *is* getting angry. (singular)
- The **jury** *has* finally reached a decision. (singular)
- The **majority** *rules* most of the time. (plural)
- The **staff** *have* gone their separate ways for the holidays. (plural)

Inverted Subjects

Here are some examples of subject verb agreement with inverted subjects where the subject follows the verb:

- There *are* seven clean **plates** in the dining room.
- There *is* a **hair** in my lasagna.

- Over the rainbow *flies* a **bird**.
- How *are* the **employees** enjoying the new building?
- A good gift *is* a **gift card**.

Suffix

What is a suffix?

A suffix is a word ending. It is a group of letters you can add to the *end* of a root word.

EXAMPLE:
- *walking*
- *helpful*

A root word stands on its own as a word, but you can make new words from it by adding beginnings (prefixes) and endings (suffixes). For example, 'comfort' is a root word. By adding the prefix 'dis' and the suffix 'able' you can make new words such as 'discomfort' and 'comfortable'.

Adding suffixes to words can change or add to their meaning, but most importantly they show how a word will be used in a sentence and what part of speech (e.g. noun, verb, adjective) the word belongs to. e.g. If you want to use the root word 'talk' in the following sentence: *I was (talk) to Samina*. You need to add the suffix 'ing' so that the word 'talk' makes better sense grammatically: *"I was talking to Samina"*.

There are various suffixes we use. Probably the most common are 'ed' and 'ing'. Here are some other suffixes and examples.

Suffix Spelling Rules - Double Letters

Usually when you add a suffix to a root word the spelling of both stays the same: e.g. care + ful = careful But there are several important groups of words where the spelling of the root word *changes* when you add a suffix.

Sometimes the spelling changes because of the **'Doubling' rules.** As always, there are exceptions to these 4 rules, but they are a good starting guide:

RULE 1.
For most short (one syllable) words that end in a single consonant (anything but 'a', 'e', 'i', 'o', 'u') you need to double the last letter when you add a suffix: e.g. run + ing = running sun + y = sunny If the word ends with more than one consonant, you don't double the last letter: e.g. pump + ed = pumped sing + ing = singing

RULE 2.
For most longer (more than one syllable) words that end in 'l' you need to double the 'l' when you add the suffix: e.g. travel + ing = traveling cancel + ed = cancelled

RULE 3.
For most longer (more than one syllable) words that have the stress on the last syllable when you say them AND end in a single consonant (anything but 'a', 'e', 'i', 'o', 'u') you need to double the last letter: e.g. begin + er = beginner prefer + ing = preferring If the word has more than one syllable and ends in

a single consonant, but the stress isn't on the last syllable, then you don't need to double the last letter before adding a suffix: e.g. offer + ing = offering benefit + ed = benefited

RULE 4.

If you have a word ending in a consonant and a suffix starting in a consonant, you don't need to double the last letter of the word: e.g. enrol + ment = enrolment commit + ment = commitment

Suffix Example

Suffix	Word		Suffix		Result
ed	walk	+	ed	=	walked
ing	say	+	ing	=	saying
er	tall	+	er	=	taller
tion	educate	+	tion	=	education
sion	divide	+	sion	=	division
cian	music	+	cian	=	musician
fully	hope	+	fully	=	hopefully
est	large	+	est	=	largest
ness	happy	+	ness	=	happiness
al	accident	+	al	=	accidental
ary	imagine	+	ary	=	imaginary
able	accept	+	able	=	acceptable
ly	love	+	ly	=	lovely
ment	excite	+	ment	=	excitement
ful	help	+	ful	=	helpful
y	ease	+	y	=	easy

More suffix spelling rules:

'Y' TO 'I' RULE

- When you add a suffix to a word which ends in a consonant followed by a 'y', change the 'y' to 'i'.

EXAMPLE:

The word 'happy' ends in 'py'. When you add the suffix 'ness', change the 'y' to 'i' to make the word happiness: happy + ness = happiness.

Exceptions to the rule.
If you are adding the suffix 'ing' to a word ending in 'y', keep the 'y'. e.g. The word 'copy' ends in 'py'. When you add 'ing' the 'y' doesn't change to an 'i' because you would have 2 'i's together: copy + ing = copying.

SILENT 'E' RULE

- When you add a 'y' or a suffix which starts with a vowel (a,e,i,o,u) to a word which ends in a silent 'e', drop the silent 'e'.

Silent 'e' words are ones that end with a consonant and have an 'e' at the end, such as hope, like, love. If you say the word to yourself you don't really hear the 'e' at the end.

EXAMPLE:

The word 'noise' ends in a silent 'e'. When you add the suffix 'y', the 'e' is dropped to make the word, noisy: noise + y = noisy. The word 'like' ends in a silent 'e'. When you add the suffix 'ing', the 'e' is dropped to make the word, liking: like + ing = liking.

Exceptions to the rule.

If a word ends in 'ce', or 'ge', keep the 'e' if you add a suffix beginning with either an 'a', or an 'o'. (This is done to keep the 'c' or 'g' sounding soft.) e.g. The word 'peace' ends in 'ce'. When you add on the suffix 'able' the silent 'e' is kept to make the word, peaceable: peace + able = peaceable

NB: All these rules also apply to words which have a prefix before the root word.

For example if you add the suffix 'ness' to the root word 'unhappy' you would still change the 'y' to 'i': un + happy + ness = unhappiness

Verbs, nouns and professions

Adding a suffix to a word can change the job that word does. There are several forms of the 'shun' sound which are all suffixes that can change root words from nouns to verbs, or give you important clues about what the word is doing.

Topic Sentence

Writing Effective Topic Sentences

What's a Topic Sentence Anyway?

The best way to understand the role of the topic sentence in paragraph development is to imagine that any given paragraph is a sort of 'mini-essay' that has its own mini-thesis, mini-support, and mini-conclusion. In fact, the parts of a paragraph correspond to the parts of an essay as follows:

Essay Level	Paragraph Level
Thesis statement →	Topic sentence
Body paragraphs →	Supporting details, explanations, analysis
Conclusion →	Wrap-up/transition sentence

Just as an effective essay starts off with an introduction that presents the paper's thesis statement and indicates the specific claim or argument that the essay will develop, so too each paragraph begins with a topic sentence that indicates the focus of that paragraph, alerting the reader to the particular *subtopic* that the paragraph will illustrate, analyze and/or explain.

The topic sentence does not *have* to be the first sentence in the paragraph; however, it should come early in the paragraph in order to orient the reader to the paragraph's focus right away. For instance, some paragraphs may begin with a transition sentence that serves to ease continuity from the previous paragraph's topic onto the current paragraph's topic. In the case of the first sentence being a transition, the topic sentence is usually the second sentence in the paragraph.

What makes an effective topic sentence?

Just as an effective thesis statement defines the paper's focus as specifically as possible, an effective topic sentence states the focus of the paragraph clearly and concisely. The remainder of the paragraph then functions to develop the point stated in the topic sentence. Consider my previous paragraph as an example:

The topic sentence does not have to be the first sentence in the paragraph; however, it should come early in the paragraph in order to orient the reader to the paragraph's focus right away. For instance, some paragraphs may begin with a transition sentence that serves to ease continuity from the previous paragraph's topic onto the current paragraph's topic. In the case of the first sentence being a transition, the topic sentence is usually the second sentence in the paragraph.

Notice how the topic sentence (italicized above) lets the reader know exactly what he or she can expect to read about in the paragraph: it's going to be a paragraph about the location of topic sentences. Moreover, every sentence within the paragraph connects back to the topic sentence through illustration, explanation or analysis; every sentence in the sample paragraph tells us something about the placement of topic sentences.

Although it may be tempting to begin a paragraph with a compelling quote, as a general rule topic sentences should state the main idea of the paragraph *in your own words*. Direct quotes have a place later in the paragraph where they may be incorporated to support the topic sentence's point.

Where can I get more information?

If you are finding it challenging to create nice, focused topic sentences, you might consider outlining before beginning to write a paper. The points and subpoints of an outline—especially if you put together a formal outline written in full sentences—can then become the topic sentences for the paper's paragraphs.

Verbs

A verb is an action word, Luv Is a Verb, Everything's a Verb, where does it end? The concept of verbs is sort of a tricky one to grasp, and then once you do, verbs only get more confusing.

Regular verbs are the ones that follow a pattern when they're changed to a different person or tense. They have up to 4 different forms: root, third-person singular present (which is usually the same as the root but with the -s added at the end), present participle, and past and past participle (which are the same).

- *Need – needs – needing – needed – needed*

Notice how the past and past participle are the same form.

- *Talk – talks – talking – talked – talked*
- *Call – calls – calling – called – called*
- *Add – adds – adding – added – added*
- *Work – works – working – worked – worked*

Present tense regular verbs don't have -s (or -es) added to the end of the root word for anything except the third-person singular.

- *My cat does whatever he wants, not what I want him to do.*
- *They shop at the big market, but he shops at the little one.*

Regular verbs also have -ed (or -d if the verb already ends in -e) added to them to change them into past tense.

- *Laugh – laughed*
- *Push – pushed*
- *Rest – rested*

Writing Process

Stages of the Writing Process

"Writing is a fluid process created by writers as they work. Accomplished writers move back and forth between the stages of the process, both consciously and unconsciously. Young writers, however, benefit from the structure and security of following the writing process in their writing.

- **Prewriting.** *Students generate ideas for writing:* brainstorming; reading literature; creating life maps, webs, and story charts; developing word banks; deciding on form, audience, voice, and purpose as well as through teacher motivation.

- **Rough Draft.** *Students get their ideas on paper.* They write without concern for conventions. Written work does not have to be neat; it is a 'sloppy copy.'

- **Reread.** *Students proof their own work* by reading aloud and reading for sensibility.

- **Share with a Peer Revisor.** *Students share and make suggestions for improvement:* asking who, what, when, where, why, and how questions about parts of the story the peer does not understand; looking for better words; and talking about how to make the work better.

- **Revise.** *Improve what the narrative says and how it says it:* write additions, imagery, and details. Take out unnecessary work. Use peer suggestions to improve. Clarify.

- **Editing.** *Work together on editing for mechanics and spelling.* Make sure the work is 'goof proof.'

- **Final Draft.** *Students produce their final copy* to discuss with the teacher and write a final draft.

CHAPTER 3

MATHEMATICS

Math·e·mat·ics

maTH(ə)ˈmadiks/

noun

noun: mathematics; noun: applied mathematics; noun: pure mathematics

- the abstract science of number, quantity, and space. Mathematics may be studied in its own right (pure mathematics), or as it is applied to other disciplines such as physics and engineering (applied mathematics).
- the mathematical aspects of something.plural noun: mathematics "the mathematics of general relativity"

Addition

Addition is finding the total, or sum, by combining two or more numbers.

EXAMPLE:

$5 + 11 + 3 = 19$ is an addition

$$8 + 3 = 11$$
Addend   Addend   Sum

Subtraction

What Is Subtraction?

Subtraction in mathematics means you are taking something away from a group or number of things. When you subtract, what is left in the group becomes less.

An example of a subtraction problem is the following:

5 - 3 = 2

Notice that there are three parts to the subtraction problem shown. The part you start with is called the **minuend**. The part being taken away is called the **subtrahend**. The part that is left after subtraction is called the **difference**. In the problem 5 - 3 = 2, the number '5' is the minuend, the number '3' is the subtrahend and the number '2' is the difference.

How Do Addition And Subtraction Compare?

Addition and subtraction are closely linked. Although addition is the opposite of subtraction, it is also true that every addition problem can be rewritten as a subtraction problem. For example, the problem 3 + 2 = 5 can be rewritten as the subtraction problem 5 - 3 = 2 or 5 - 2 = 3. Notice that the sum '5' in the addition problem became the minuend and the other numbers became the subtrahend and the difference.

In addition, you probably learned something like the following: if 3 + 2 = 5, then 2 + 3 = 5. In other words, you can change the order of the numbers you add and get the same answer. This cannot be done in subtraction. For example, 5 - 3 and 3 - 5 do not equal the same value.

Methods Of Subtraction

One method of subtraction is to use a diagram showing what you start with, what you are taking away and what you are left with.

EXAMPLE

The problem 5 - 3 might be described with following diagram:

Subtraction is ...

... taking one number away from another.

Start with *5 apples*,
then *subtract 2*,
we are left with *3 apples*.

This can be written: **5 − 2 = 3**

Mixed Operations

Order of Operations - PEMDAS

Operations

"Operations" means things like add, subtract, multiply, divide, squaring, etc. If it isn't a number it is probably an operation.

But, when you see something like:
$7 + (6 \times 5^2 + 3)$

What part should you calculate first? Start at the left and go to the right? Or go from right to left?

Warning: *Calculate them in the wrong order, and you will get a wrong answer!*

So, long ago people agreed to follow rules when doing calculations, and they are:

Order of Operations

Do things in Parentheses First.

EXAMPLE:

6 × (5 + 3) = 6 × 8 = 48 ✓
6 × (5 + 3) = 30 + 3 = 33 *(wrong)*

Exponents (Powers, Roots) before Multiply, Divide, Add or Subtract.

EXAMPLE:

5 × 2² = 5 × 4 = 20 ✓
5 × 2² = 10² = 100 *(wrong)*

Multiply or Divide before you Add or Subtract.

EXAMPLE:

2 + 5 × 3 = 2 + 15 = 17 ✓
2 + 5 × 3 = 7 × 3 = 21 *(wrong)*

Otherwise just go left to right.

EXAMPLE:

30 ÷ 5 × 3 = 6 × 3 = 18 ✓
30 ÷ 5 × 3 = 30 ÷ 15 = 2 *(wrong)*

How Do I Remember It All?

PEMDAS !

- **P**   Parentheses first
- **E**   Exponents (ie Powers and Square Roots, etc.)
- **MD**   Multiplication and Division (left-to-right)
- **AS**   Addition and Subtraction (left-to-right)

Estimating & Rounding

- Rounding makes numbers that are easier to work with in your head.

- Rounded numbers are only approximate.

- An exact answer generally can not be obtained using rounded numbers.

- Use rounding to get a answer that is close but that does not have to be exact.

- How to round numbers

- Make the numbers that end in 1 through 4 into the next lower number that ends in 0. For example 74 rounded to the nearest ten would be 70.

- Numbers that end in a digit of 5 or more should be rounded up to the next even ten. The number 88 rounded to the nearest ten would be 90.

Rounding Numbers

A rounded number has *about the same value* as the number you start with, but it is *less exact.*

For example, 341 rounded to the nearest hundred is 300. That is because 341 is closer in value to 300 than to 400. When rounding off to the nearest dollar, $1.89 becomes $2.00, because $1.89 is closer to $2.00 than to $1.00

Rules for Rounding

Here's the general rule for rounding:

- If the number you are rounding is followed by 5, 6, 7, 8, or 9, round the number up.

EXAMPLE:

38 rounded to the nearest ten is 40!

- If the number you are rounding is followed by 0, 1, 2, 3, or 4, round the number down.

EXAMPLE:

33 rounded to the nearest ten is 30

What Are You Rounding to?

When rounding a number, you first need to ask: *what are you rounding it to?* Numbers can be rounded to the nearest ten, the nearest hundred, the nearest thousand, and so on.

Consider the number 4,827.

- 4,827 rounded to the nearest ten is 4,830
- 4,827 rounded to the nearest hundred is 4,800
- 4,827 rounded to the nearest thousand is 5,000

All the numbers to the right of the place you are rounding to become zeros. Here are some more examples:

- 34 rounded to the nearest ten is 30
- 6,809 rounded to the nearest hundred is 6,800
- 1,951 rounded to the nearest thousand is 2,000

Rounding and Fractions

Rounding fractions *works exactly the same way* as rounding whole numbers. The only difference is that instead of rounding to tens, hundreds, thousands, and so on, you round to tenths, hundredths, thousandths, and so on.

- 7.8199 rounded to the nearest tenth is 7.8
- 1.0621 rounded to the nearest hundredth is 1.06
- 3.8792 rounded to the nearest thousandth is 3.879

Here's a tip: to *avoid getting confused* in rounding long decimals, *look only at the number in the place you are rounding to and the number that follows it.* For example, to round 5.3824791401 to the nearest hundredth, just look at the number in the hundredths place—8—and the number that follows it—2. Then you can easily round it to 5.38.

Rounding and Sums

Rounding can *make sums easy.* For example, at a grocery store you might pick up items with the following prices:

- $2.25
- $0.88
- $2.69

If you wanted to know about how much they would cost, you could add up the prices with a pen and paper, or try to add them in your head. Or you could do it the simple way—you could estimate by rounding off to the nearest dollar, like this:

- $2.00
- $1.00
- $3.00

By rounding off, you could easily figure out that you would need about $6.00 to pay for your groceries. This is pretty close to the exact number of $5.82.

As you can see, in finding a round sum, it is quickest to *round the numbers before adding them.*

Probability

Probability
*How **likely** something is to happen.*

Many events can't be predicted with total certainty. The best we can say is how *likely* they are to happen, using the idea of probability.

Tossing a Coin

When a coin is tossed, there are two possible outcomes:

- heads (H)
- tails (T)

We say that the probability of the coin landing *H is ½.* And the probability of the coin landing *T is ½.*

Throwing Dice
When a single die is thrown, there are six possible outcomes:

- 1, 2, 3, 4, 5, 6.

The probability of any one of them is 1/6.

Probability

In general:

$$\text{Probability of an event happening} = \frac{\text{Number of ways it can happen}}{\text{Total number of outcomes}}$$

EXAMPLE:

The chances of rolling a "4" with a die.

Number of ways it can happen: **1**
(there is only 1 face with a "4" on it)

Total number of outcomes: **6**
(there are 6 faces altogether)

So the probability = 1/6

EXAMPLE:

there are 5 marbles in a bag: 4 are blue, and 1 is red. What is the probability that a blue marble gets picked?

Number of ways it can happen: **4**
(there are 4 blues)

Total number of outcomes: **5**
(there are 5 marbles in total)

So the probability = 4/5 = 0.8

Probability Line

We can show probability on a Probability Line:

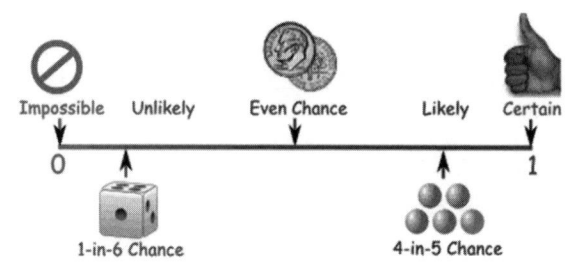

Probability is always between 0 and 1

Probability is Just a Guide

Probability does not tell us exactly what will happen, it is just a guide.

EXAMPLE:

Toss a coin 100 times, how many Heads will come up?

Probability says that heads have a ½ chance, so we can *expect 50 Heads.*

But when we actually try it we might get 48 heads, or 55 heads ... or anything really, but in most cases it will be a number near 50.

Stem and Leaf Plots

A Stem and Leaf Plot is a special table where each data value is split into a "stem" (the first digit or digits) and a "leaf" (usually the last digit). Like in this example:

EXAMPLE:

"32" is split into "3" (stem) and "2" (leaf).

15, 16, 21, 23, 23, 26, 26, 30, 32, 41

Stem	Leaf
1	5 6
2	1 3 3 6 6
3	0 2
4	1

how to place "32"

Stem "1" Leaf "5" means 15

Graphing

Let's draw the graph of this equation.

$$y = \tfrac{1}{2} x + 2$$

One method we could use is to find the x and y values of two points that satisfy the equation, plot each point, and then draw a line through the points. We can start with any two x values we like, and then find y for each x by substituting the x values into the equation. Let's start with x = 1.

Value of x	$y = \tfrac{1}{2} x + 2$	Value of y
1	$y = \tfrac{1}{2} \cdot 1 + 2 = \tfrac{1}{2} + 2$	2.5
2	$y = \tfrac{1}{2} \cdot 2 + 2 = 1 + 2$	3

Let's plot these points and draw a line through them.

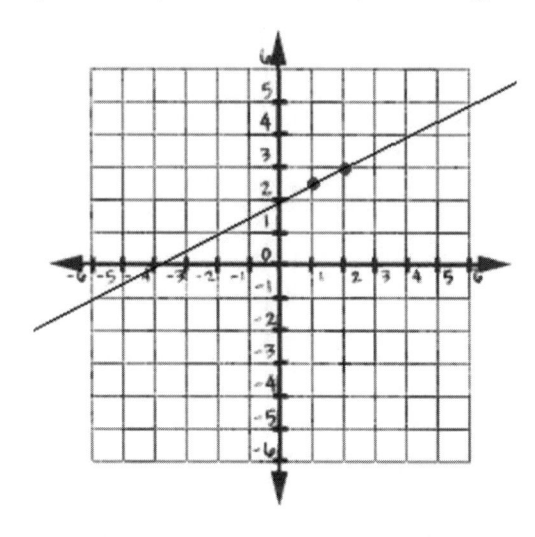

Graphing Using Slope and Y-Intercept There's another way to graph an equation using your knowledge of slope and y-intercept. Look at the equation again.

$$y = mx + b$$
$$y = \tfrac{1}{2} x + 2$$

We can find the slope and y-intercept of the line just by looking at the equation: m = 1/2 and y intercept = 2.

Just by looking at these values, we already know one point on the line! The y-intercept gives us the point where the line intersects the y-axis, so we know the coordinates of that point are (0, 2), since the x value of any point that lies on the y axis is zero.

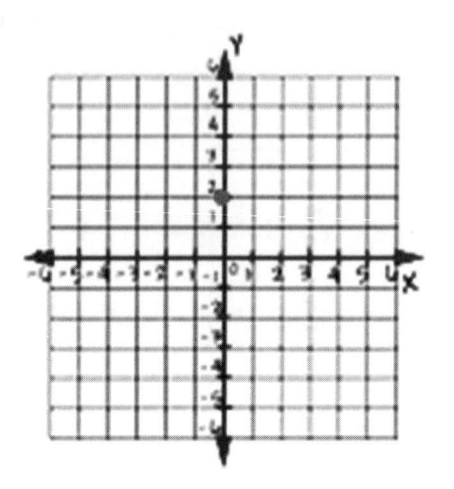

To find the second point, we can use the slope of the line. The slope is ½, which gives us the change in the y value over the change in the x value. The change in the x value, the denominator, is 2, so we move to the right 2 units.

The change in the y value, the numerator, is positive one. We move up one unit. This gives us the second point we need. Now we can draw the line through the points.

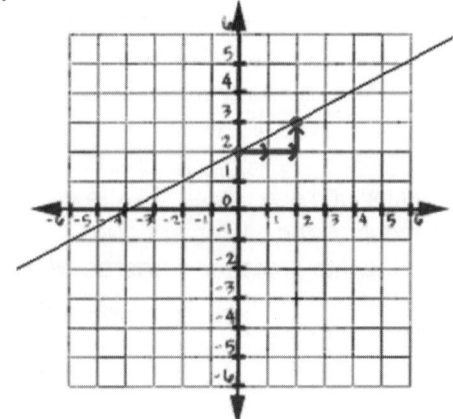

This is the exact same line we found using the first method. Do you see that it's quicker and easier to use the y-intercept and the slope? You can use either method to graph the line, depending on what information you have about the line and its equation.

Length

Metric Length

We can measure how long things are, or how tall, or how far apart they are. Those are are all examples of length measurements.

Example: This fork is 20 centimeters long

These are the most common measurements:
- Millimeters
- Centimeters
- Meters
- Kilometers

Small units of length are called **millimeters**.
- A millimeter is about the thickness of a plastic id card (or credit card).
- Or about the thickness of 10 sheets of paper on top of each other.

This is a very small measurement!

When we have 10 millimeters, it can be called a **centimeter.**

1 centimeter = 10 millimeters

- A fingernail is about one centimeter wide.

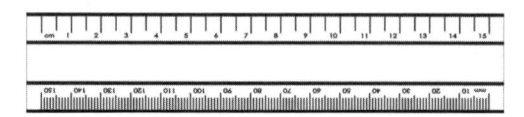

Two tape measures, one in mm, the other in cm

We can use millimeters or centimeters to measure how tall we are, or how wide a table is, but to measure the length of football field it is better to use **meters.**

1 meter = 100 centimeters

- The length of this guitar is about 1 meter

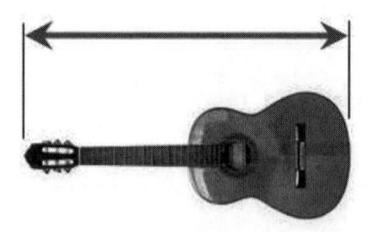

Meters might be used to measure the length of a house, or the size of a playground.

And because a centimeter is 10 millimeters:

1 meter = 1000 millimeters

1 kilometer = 1000 meters

When we need to get from one place to another, we measure the distance using **kilometers.**

The distance from one city to another or how far a plane travels can be measured using kilometers.

Final thoughts about measuring length:

- **1 centimeter = 10 millimeters**
- **1 meter = 100 centimeters**
- **1 kilometer = 1000 meters**

LOTS OF EXAMPLES:

A centimeter (cm) is about:

- about as long as a staple
- the width of a highlighter
- the diameter of a belly button
- the width of 5 CD's stacked on top of each other
- the thickness of a notepad.
- the radius (half the diameter) of a US penny

A meter (m) is about:

- a little more than a yard (1 yard is exactly 0.9144 meters)
- the width of a doorway (most doorways are about 0.8 to 0.9 m)
- half the length of a bed
- the width of a large fridge
- the height of a countertop
- four rungs up a ladder

- five steps up a staircase
- the depth of the shallow end of a swimming pool
- the width of a dining table
- the height of a 5 year old
- shoulder to opposite wrist of an adult
- outstreched arms of a child
- waist high on an adult

Length

- *One meter equals* roughly one long step of an adult man.
- *A kilometer (km) is* a little over half a mile
- *A Kilometer is* a quarter of the average depth of the ocean
- *One kilometer equals* about 12 minutes' walk

Mass

Weight or Mass?

Q: Aren't "weight" and "mass" the same?

A: Not really.

An object *has mass* (say 100 kg). This makes it heavy enough to show a weight of "100 kg".

Gravity causes Weight

An objects weight is how hard gravity is pulling on it.

We think the weight is the same everywhere because we all live on the surface of the planet Earth!

But in orbit it would not push on the scales at all.

The scales would show **0 kg**... but the mass is still **100 kg**!

An object's **mass doesn't change** *(unless you remove some!)*, but its **weight can change.**

So Why Do People Say Weight instead of Mass?

People often use "weight" to mean "mass", and vice versa. Because gravity is pretty much the same everywhere on Earth, we don't notice a difference. But remember, they do not mean the same thing, and they can have different measurements.

Here are some conditions where the Weight might change:

- in space (can be weightless!)
- on the moon (a 100 kg mass would weigh 16.6 kg)
- you can even get very slight differences in weight in different locations on earth!

Weight is a Force

So, if weight and mass are different, why are they both in kilograms? Well, weight should not really be in kilograms! I have used "kilogram" so far because that is what you would see on a pair of scales, but it is technically *wrong to talk about weight in kilograms.*

There is a better measurement: **Newtons**

Newtons

The correct *unit* for force is the **Newton** (=1 kg•m/s2) which is abbreviated **N**.

Gravity makes a 1 kilogram **mass** exert about 9.8 Newtons of **force**.

So a 100kg mass really weighs about 980 Newtons on Earth.

Why Scales Show Kilograms or Pounds

Scales show Kilograms or Pounds because that is what people understand best. It is really just an **estimate of the mass above them.** Scales should really show Newtons, but that might confuse people!

QUESTION:
How many Newtons should the scales show when you stand on them (hint: multiply kg by 9.8)?

So the scales show an **estimate of your mass** based on the force your body exerts on it.

To find out how much force your body is exerting on the scales, multiply by 9.8 (to convert kg into Newtons).

Apparent Weight

But Scales can be fooled ... because they measure a "downwards force" and don't know if it is gravity or some other force!

Just jump up and down (gently!) on your scales at home to see your apparent weight change, while your mass stays the same.

So your **mass** is the same, and your **weight** is the same (because the force of gravity hasn't changed), but your **"apparent" weight changes.**

Conclusion

- **Mass** is a measure of how much matter something contains
- **Weight** is a measure of how strongly gravity pulls downwards
- **Apparent Weight** is a measure of downwards force
- **Force** is measured in **Newtons**, not kilograms or pounds
- When scales show "kg" or "lb" it is just an estimate of the mass above them

Volume

3 × 3 × 3 = 27

There are 27 cubic feet in a cubic yard.

Try to count the 1 ft cubes below, and you will see why:

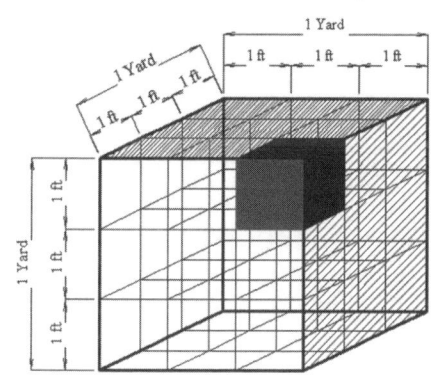

EXAMPLE:
Convert 30 cubic feet into cubic meters
(30 ft³ to m³)

The conversion for feet to meters is:

1 ft = 0.3048 m

So, the length conversion is to multiply by 0.3048 And the Volume Conversion must be to multiply by 0.3048, and multiply by 0.3048 and multiply by 0.3048 again:

30 × 0.3048 × 0.3048 × 0.3048 = 0.85

So, 30 ft3 = 0.85 m3

Time

Time - AM/PM vs 24 Hour Clock

Normally the time is shown as **Hours:Minutes**

There are 24 Hours in a Day and 60 Minutes in each Hour.

EXAMPLE:
10:25 means 10 Hours and 25 Minutes

Showing the Time
There are two main ways to show the time:

"24 Hour Clock" or "AM/PM":

24 Hour Clock: the time is shown as how many hours and minutes since midnight.

AM/PM (or "12 Hour Clock"): the day is split into:

- the 12 Hours running from Midnight to Noon (the AM hours)

- the other 12 Hours running from Noon to Midnight (the PM hours)

Like this (24-hour above and AM/PM below it):

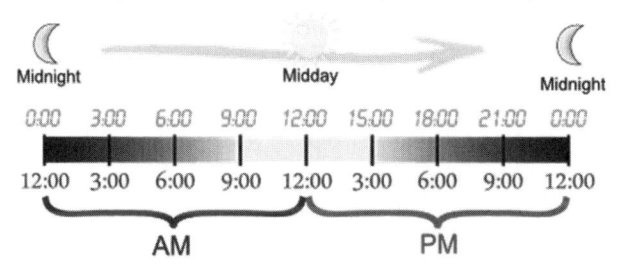

```
☾                                              ☾
Midnight            Midday                Midnight
0:00   3:00  6:00  9:00  12:00 15:00 18:00 21:00 0:00

12:00  3:00  6:00  9:00  12:00  3:00  6:00  9:00  12:00
      _____/      _____/
              AM                      PM
```

	AM	**PM**
	Ante Meridiem* *Latin for* *"before midday"*	**Post Meridiem*** *Latin for* *"after midday"*
When:	**Midnight to Noon**	**Noon to Midnight**
24 Hr Clock:	0:00 to 11:59	12:00 to 23:59

Converting AM/PM to 24 Hour Clock

- Add 12 to any hour after Noon (and subtract 12 for the first hour of the day)

- For the first hour of the day (12 Midnight to 12:59 AM), subtract 12 Hours

EXAMPLES:
12 Midnight = 0:00, 12:35 AM = 0:35
From 1:00 AM to 12:59 PM, no change

EXAMPLES:
11:20 AM = 11:20, 12:30 PM = 12:30
From 1:00 PM to 11:59 PM, add 12 Hours

EXAMPLES:
4:45 PM = 16:45, 11:50 PM = 23:50

Converting 24 Hour Clock to AM/PM
For the first hour of the day (0:00 to 0:59), add 12 Hours, make it "AM"

EXAMPLES:
0:10 = 12:10 AM, 0:40 = 12:40 AM
From 1:00 to 11:59, just make it "AM"

EXAMPLES:
1:15 = 1:15 AM, 11:25 = 11:25 AM
From 12:00 to 12:59, just make it "PM"

EXAMPLES:
12:10 = 12:10 PM, 12:55 = 12:55 PM
From 13:00 to 23:59, subtract 12 Hours, make it "PM"

EXAMPLES:
14:55 = 2:55 PM, 23:30 = 11:30 PM

Comparison Chart

Here is a side-by-side comparison of the 24 Hour Clock and AM/PM:

EXAMPLE: on the hour		EXAMPLE: 10 minutes past	
24 Hour Clock	**AM / PM**	**24 Hour Clock**	**AM / PM**
0:00	12 Midnight	0:10	12:10 AM
1:00	1:00 AM	1:10	1:10 AM
2:00	2:00 AM	2:10	2:10 AM
3:00	3:00 AM	3:10	3:10 AM
4:00	4:00 AM	4:10	4:10 AM
5:00	5:00 AM	5:10	5:10 AM
6:00	6:00 AM	6:10	6:10 AM
7:00	7:00 AM	7:10	7:10 AM
8:00	8:00 AM	8:10	8:10 AM
9:00	9:00 AM	9:10	9:10 AM
10:00	10:00 AM	10:10	10:10 AM
11:00	11:00 AM	11:10	11:10 AM
12:00	**12 Noon**	**12:10**	**12:10 PM**
13:00	1:00 PM	13:10	1:10 PM
14:00	2:00 PM	14:10	2:10 PM
15:00	3:00 PM	15:10	3:10 PM
16:00	4:00 PM	16:10	4:10 PM
17:00	5:00 PM	17:10	5:10 PM
18:00	6:00 PM	18:10	6:10 PM
19:00	7:00 PM	19:10	7:10 PM
20:00	8:00 PM	20:10	8:10 PM
21:00	9:00 PM	21:10	9:10 PM
22:00	10:00 PM	22:10	10:10 PM
23:00	11:00 PM	23:10	11:10 PM

Midnight and Noon

"12 AM" and "12 PM" can cause confusion, so we prefer "12 Midnight" and "12 Noon".

What Day is Midnight?
Midnight has another problem: there is nothing to tell us "is this the beginning or ending of the day".

Multiplication

Multiplication means times (or repeated addition). The symbol used for multiplication is '×'.

EXAMPLE:

4 × 6 = 24

This is read as four times six is equal to twenty-four or simply, four times six is twenty-four.

Note: Knowledge of multiplication is very important. So, if you are weak in multiplication, you must try to attain a proficiency in the following 'times table'.

×	1	2	3	4	5	6	7	8	9	10
1	1	2	3	4	5	6	7	8	9	10
2	2	4	6	8	10	12	14	16	18	20
3	3	6	9	12	15	18	21	24	27	30
4	4	8	12	16	20	24	28	32	36	40
5	5	10	15	20	25	30	35	40	45	50
6	6	12	18	24	30	36	42	48	54	60
7	7	14	21	28	35	42	49	56	63	70
8	8	16	24	32	40	48	56	64	72	80
9	9	18	27	36	45	54	63	72	81	90
10	10	20	30	40	50	60	70	80	90	100

Your confidence and ability to learn mathematics will depend largely on your knowledge of multiplication. So, you should aim to master this 'times table'.

Whole Numbers and Integers

Whole Numbers

Whole Numbers are simply the numbers 0, 1, 2, 3, 4, 5, ... (and so on)

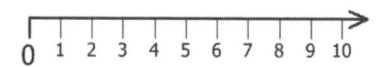

```
0  1  2  3  4  5  6  7  8  9  10
```

No Fractions!

Counting Numbers

Counting Numbers are Whole Numbers, but **without the zero.** Because you can't "count" zero.

So they are **1, 2, 3, 4, 5,** ... (and so on).

Natural Numbers

"Natural Numbers" can mean either "Counting Numbers" {1, 2, 3, ...}, or "Whole Numbers" {0, 1, 2, 3, ...}, depending on the subject.

Integers

Integers are like whole numbers, but they **also include negative numbers**...but still no fractions allowed!

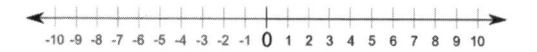

```
-10 -9 -8 -7 -6 -5 -4 -3 -2 -1  0  1  2  3  4  5  6  7  8  9  10
```

So, integers can be negative {-1, -2,-3, -4, -5, ... }, positive {1, 2, 3, 4, 5, ... }, or zero {0}

We can put that all together like this:

Integers = { ..., -5, -4, -3, -2, -1, 0, 1, 2, 3, 4, 5, ... }

EXAMPLE:
These are all integers:

-16, -3, 0, 1, 198

(But numbers like ½, 1.1 and 3.5 are **not** integers)

Division

Division is splitting into equal parts or groups. It is the result of "fair sharing".

EXAMPLE:
There are 12 chocolates, and 3 friends want to share them, how do they divide the chocolates?

12 Chocolates   *12 Chocolates Divided by 3*

ANSWER:
12 divided by 3 is 4: they get 4 each

Symbols

÷ /

We use the ÷ symbol, or sometimes the / symbol to mean divide:

12 ÷ 3 = 4   12 / 3 = 4

Let's use both symbols here so we get used to them.

Opposite of Multiplying

Division is the opposite of multiplying. When we know a multiplication fact we can find a division fact:

EXAMPLE:

3 × 5 = 15, so 15 / 5 = 3
Also 15 / 3 = 5

Why? Well, think of the numbers in rows and columns like in this illustration:

Multiplication:
3 groups of 5 make 15.

Division:
so 15 divided by 3 is 5

and also:

5 groups of 3 make 15

...so 15 divided by 5 is 3.

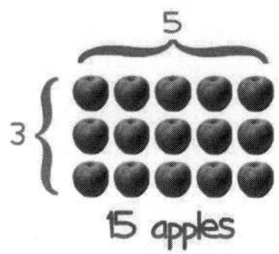

So there are four related facts:

- 3 × 5 = 15
- 5 × 3 = 15
- 15 / 3 = 5
- 15 / 5 = 3

Knowing your Multiplication Tables can help you with division!

EXAMPLE:

What is 28 ÷ 7 ?

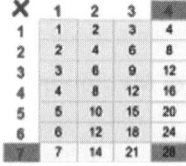

Searching around the multiplication table we find that 28 is 4 × 7, so 28 divided by 7 must be 4.

ANSWER:

28 ÷ 7 = 4

Names

There are special names for each number in a division:

dividend ÷ divisor = quotient

EXAMPLE:

in 12 ÷ 3 = 4:

- 12 is the dividend
- 3 is the divisor
- 4 is the quotient

But Sometimes It Does Not Work Perfectly!

Sometimes we cannot divide things up evenly, there may be something left over.

EXAMPLE:

There are 7 bones to share with 2 pups. But 7 cannot be divided exactly into 2 groups, so each pup gets 3 bones, but there will be 1 left over:

7 ÷ 2 = 3 R 1 ← Remainder

We call that the Remainder.

Long Division

Introduction

$10

John and Ann are given $10 to share. How do they share it? Easy! $5 each.

$5
$5

But then they think of their little baby brother Max.

"Maybe we should share it with him?" they ask each other.

So how much do they each get?

$10 shared amongst 3 people

That is $3 each ... but 3 lots of $3 is $9:

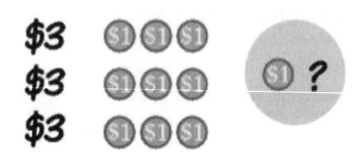

$3 $1 $1 $1
$3 $1 $1 $1 $1 ?
$3 $1 $1 $1

That leaves $1 still to share.

Let us break that $1 into ten 10c pieces:

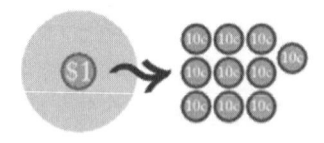

OK. Let's share those 10 cent pieces. That is 30 cents each:

$3.30 $1 $1 $1 10c 10c 10c
$3.30 $1 $1 $1 10c 10c 10c   10c ?
$3.30 $1 $1 $1 10c 10c 10c

But that still leaves 10c !!!

So let us turn the 10c into ten 1c pieces:

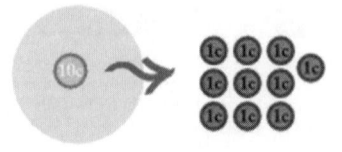

OK, share that too: they each get 3c:

$3.33
$3.33
$3.33

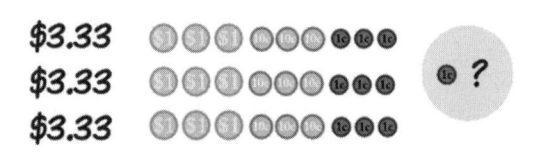

That leaves one cent! But we can't break that cent any further so it is simply "left over", which we call the "remainder"

THE ANSWER IS:

They each get $3 and another 30c and another 3c and then one cent left over!

$3.33 each (with a remainder of 1c)

Fractions

Adding Fractions

There are 3 Simple Steps to add fractions:

STEP 1.
Make sure the bottom numbers (the denominators) are the same.

STEP 2.
Add the top numbers (the numerators), put the answer over the denominator.

STEP 3.
Simplify the fraction (if needed)

EXAMPLE 1:

$\frac{1}{4} + \frac{1}{4}$

STEP 1.

The bottom numbers (the denominators) are already the same. Go straight to step 2.

STEP 2.

Add the top numbers and put the answer over the same denominator:

$\frac{1}{4} + \frac{1}{4} = \frac{1+1}{4} = \frac{2}{4}$

STEP 3.

Simplify the fraction:

$\frac{2}{4} = \frac{1}{2}$

In picture form it looks like this:

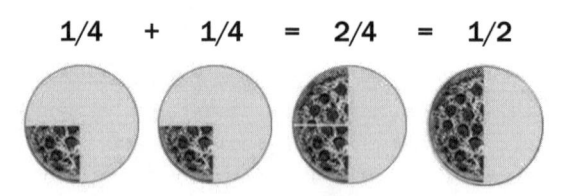

1/4 + 1/4 = 2/4 = 1/2

do you see how 2/4 is simpler as 1/2 ?

EXAMPLE 2:

$\frac{1}{3} + \frac{1}{6}$

STEP 1:

The bottom numbers are different. See how the slices are different sizes?

1/3   +   1/6   =   ?

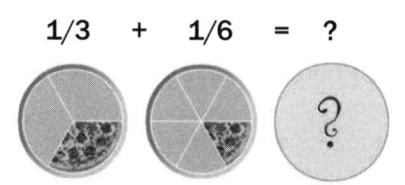

We need to make them the same before we can continue, because we **can't** add them like that.

The number "6" is twice as big as "3", so to make the bottom numbers the same we can multiply the top and bottom of the first fraction by 2, like this:

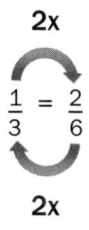

$$\frac{1}{3} = \frac{2}{6}$$

(2x top and bottom)

Important: you multiply both top and bottom by the same amount, to keep the value of the fraction the same.

Now the fractions have the same bottom number ("6"), and our question looks like this:

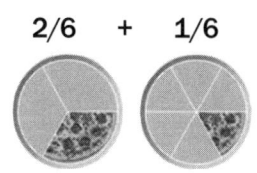

2/6   +   1/6

The bottom numbers are now the same

So we can go to step 2.

STEP 2:
Add the top numbers and put them over the same denominator:

$$\frac{2}{6} + \frac{1}{6} = \frac{2+1}{6} = \frac{3}{6}$$

In picture form it looks like this:

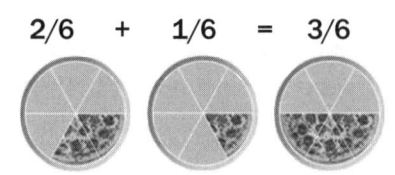

2/6   +   1/6   =   3/6

STEP 3:
Simplify the fraction:

$$\frac{3}{6} = \frac{1}{2}$$

In picture form the whole answer looks like this:

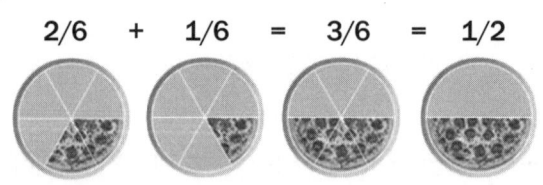

2/6   +   1/6   =   3/6   =   1/2

Decimals

Definition:

A **decimal** is any number in our base-ten number system. Specifically, we will be using numbers that have one or more digits to the right of the decimal point in this unit of lessons. The decimal point is used to separate the ones place from the tenths place in decimals. (It is also used to separate dollars from cents in money.) As we move to the right of the decimal point, each number place is divided by 10.

Below we have expressed the number $57 \frac{49}{100}$ in expanded form and in decimal form.

Mixed Number	EXPANDED FORM		Decimal Form
$57 \frac{49}{100}$	= (5x10) + (7x1)	+ (4x $\frac{1}{10}$) + (9x $\frac{1}{100}$)	= 57.49

As you can see, it is easier to write $57 \frac{49}{100}$ in decimal form. Let's look at this decimal number in a place-value chart to better understand how decimals work.

PLACE VALUE AND DECIMALS

millions	hundred thousands	ten thousands	thousands	hundreds	tens	ones	and	tenths	hundredths	thousandths	ten-thousandths	hundred-thousandths	millionths
					5	7	.	4	9				

As we move to the right in the place value chart, each number place is divided by 10. For example, thousands divided by 10 gives you hundreds. This is also true for digits to the right of the decimal point. For example, tenths divided by 10 gives you hundredths. When reading decimals, the decimal point should be read as "and." Thus, we read the decimal 57.49 as "fifty-seven and forty-nine hundredths." Note that in daily life it is common to read the decimal point as "point" instead of "and." Thus, 57.49 would be read as "fifty-seven point four nine." This usage is not considered mathematically correct.

EXAMPLE 1:

Write each phrase as a fraction and as a decimal.

Phrase	Fraction	Decimal
six tenths	$\frac{6}{10}$	.6
five hundredths	$\frac{5}{100}$	.05
thirty-two hundredths	$\frac{32}{100}$	.32
two hundred sixty-seven thousandths	$\frac{267}{1000}$	.267

So why do we use decimals?

Decimals are used in situations which require more precision than whole numbers can provide. A good example of this is money: Three and one-fourth dollars is an amount between 3 dollars and 4 dollars. We use decimals to write this amount as $3.25.

A decimal may have both a whole-number part and a fractional part. The whole-number part of a decimal are those digits to the left of the decimal point. The fractional part of a decimal is represented by the digits to the right of the decimal point. The decimal point is used to separate these parts. Let's look at some examples of this.

Decimal	Whole-Number Part	Fractional Part
3.25	3	25
4.172	4	172
25.03	25	03
0.168	0	168
132.7	132	7

Let's examine these decimals in our place-value chart.

millions	hundred thousands	ten thousands	thousands	hundreds	tens	ones	and	tenths	hundredths	thousandths	ten-thousandths	hundred-thousandths	millionths
						3	.	2	5				
						4	.	1	7	2			
					2	5	.	0	3				
						0	.	1	6	8			
				1	3	2	.	7					

Note that 0.168 has the same value as .168. However, the zero in the ones place helps us remember that 0.168 is a number less than one. From this point on, when writing a decimal that is less than one, we will always include a zero in the ones place. Let's look at some more examples of decimals.

EXAMPLE 2:
Write each phrase as a decimal.

Phrase	Decimal
fifty-six hundredths	0.560
nine tenths	0.900
thirteen and four hundredths	13.040
twenty-five and eighty-one hundredths	25.810
nineteen and seventy-eight thousandths	19.078

EXAMPLE 3:

Write each decimal using words.

Decimal	Phrase
0.0050	five thousandths
100.6000	one hundred and six tenths
2.2800	two and twenty-eight hundredths
71.0620	seventy-one and sixty-two thousandths
3.0589	three and five hundred eighty-nine ten-thousandths

It should be noted that five thousandths can also be written as zero and five thousandths.

Expanded Form

We can write the whole number 159 in expanded form as follows: 159 = (1 x 100) + (5 x 10) + (9 x 1). Decimals can also be written in expanded form. Expanded form is a way to write numbers by showing the value of each digit. This is shown in the example below.

EXAMPLE 4:

Write each decimal in expanded form.

Decimal		Expanded Form
4.1200	=	$(4 \times 1) + (1 \times \frac{1}{10}) + (2 \times \frac{1}{100})$
0.9000	=	$(0 \times 1) + (9 \times \frac{1}{10})$
9.7350	=	$(9 \times 1) + (7 \times \frac{1}{10}) + (3 \times \frac{1}{100}) + (5 \times \frac{1}{1000})$
1.0827	=	$(1 \times 1) + (0 \times \frac{1}{10}) + (8 \times \frac{1}{100}) + (2 \times \frac{1}{1000}) + (7 \times \frac{1}{10000})$

Decimal Digits

In the decimal number 1.0827, the digits 0, 8, 2 and 7 are called decimal digits.

Definition:
In a decimal number, the digits to the right of the decimal point that name the fractional part of that number, are called decimal digits.

EXAMPLE 5:

Identify the decimal digits in each decimal number below.

Decimal Number	Decimal Digits
1.4	1.**4**
359.62	359.**62**
54.0017	54.**0017**
0.729	0.**729**
63.10148	63.**10148**

Writing whole numbers as decimals

A decimal is any number, including whole numbers, in our base-ten number system. The decimal point is usually not written in whole numbers, but it is implied. For example, the whole number 4 is equivalent to the decimals 4. and 4.0. The whole number 326 is equivalent to the decimals 326. and 326.0. This important concept will be used throughout this unit.

EXAMPLE 6:

Write each whole number as a decimal.

Whole Number	Decimal	Decimal with 0
17	17.	17.0
459	459.	459.0
8	8.	8.0
1,024	1,024.	1,024.0
519	519.	519.0
63,836	63,836.	63,836.0

Often, extra zeros are written to the right of the last digit of a decimal number. These extra zeros are place holders and do not change the value of the decimal.

EXAMPLE:

7.5 = 7.50 = 7.500 = 7.5000 and so on.

9 = 9. = 9.0 = 9.00 and so on.

Note that the decimals listed above are equivalent decimals.

So how long can a decimal get?

A decimal can have any number of decimal places to the right of the decimal point. An example of a decimal number with many decimal places is the numerical value of Pi, shortened to 50 decimal digits, as shown below:

3.14159265358979323846264338
327950288 419716939937510

Summary

A decimal is any number in our base ten number system. In this lesson we used numbers that have one or more digits to the right of the decimal point. The decimal point is used to separate the whole number part from the fractional part; it is handy separator. Decimal numbers are used in situations which require more precision than whole numbers can provide. As we move to the right of the decimal point, each number place is divided by 10.

Read and Write Decimals

In the last lesson, you were introduced to decimal numbers. Decimal places change by a factor of 10. For example, let's look at the number 3,247.8956 below.

3	x	1000	thousands
2	x	100	hundreds
4	x	10	tens
7	x	1	ones
8	x	0.1	tenths
9	x	0.01	hundredths
5	x	0.001	thousandths
6	x	0.0001	ten-thousandths

A decimal number can have a whole-number part and a fractional part.

Mixed Number	EXPANDED FORM		Decimal Form
$57 \frac{49}{100}$	$= (5 \times 10) + (7 \times 1)$	$+ (4 \times \frac{1}{10}) + (9 \times \frac{1}{100})$	$= 57.49$
	Whole-Number Part	Fractional Part	

In this lesson, you will learn how to read and write decimals. You may use our Place Value and Decimals Chart (PDF) as a visual reference for the examples presented in this lesson.

EXAMPLE 1:

Write each mixed number as a decimal.

Mixed Number	Decimal
$49 \frac{1}{100}$	52.3000
$216 \frac{231}{1000}$	973.4100
$9,010 \frac{359}{10,000}$	31.2670
$76,000 \frac{47}{100,000}$	1,842.0056

EXAMPLE 2:

Write each phrase as a mixed number and as a decimal.

Phrase	Mixed Number
five and three tenths	$5 \frac{3}{10}$
forty-nine and one hundredth	$49 \frac{1}{100}$
two hundred sixteen and two hundred thirty-one thousandths	$216 \frac{231}{1000}$
nine thousand, ten and three hundred fifty-nine ten-thousandths	$9{,}010 \frac{359}{10{,}000}$
seventy-six thousand, fifty-three and forty-seven hundred-thousandths	$76{,}000 \frac{47}{100{,}000}$
two hundred twenty-nine thousand and eighty-one millionths	$229{,}000 \frac{81}{1{,}000{,}000}$

Look at the mixed numbers in the examples above. You will notice that the denominator of the fractional part is a factor of 10, making it is easy to convert to a decimal. Let's look at some examples in which the denominator is not a factor of 10.

EXAMPLE 3:

Write each mixed number as a decimal.

Analysis:

A fraction bar tells us to divide. In order to do this, we must convert or change the fractional part of each mixed number to decimal digits. We will do this by dividing the numerator of each fraction by its denominator.

Alternate Method:

It should be noted that some of the fractions above could have been converted to decimals using equivalent fractions. For example:

$$\frac{18}{20} = \frac{19}{100}$$

EXAMPLE 4:

When asked to write two hundred thousandths as a decimal, three students gave three different answers as shown below. Which student had the correct answer?

Student 1: 200,000.

Student 2: 0.200

Student 3: 0.00002

Analysis:

Let's use our place value chart to help us analyze this problem.

	millions	hundred thousands	ten thousands	thousands	hundreds	tens	ones	and	tenths	hundredths	thousandths	ten-thousandths	hundred-thousandths	millionths
Student 1		2	0	0	0	0	0	.						
Student 2							0	.	2	0	0			
Student 3							0	.	0	0	0	0	2	

Let's look at the expanded form of each decimal to help us find the correct answer.

Student	Number	Fraction	Expanded Form	Phrase
1	200,000.00000		2x100,000	two hundred thousand
2	0.20000	$\frac{200}{1,000}$	$200 \times \frac{1}{1,000}$	two hundred thousandths
3	0.00002	$\frac{2}{100,000}$	$2 \times \frac{1}{100,000}$	two hundred-thousandths

ANSWER:

Thus, two hundred thousandths is 0.200, so Student 2 had the correct answer.

As you can see, decimals are named by the place of the last digit. Notice that in Example 4, the answer given by Student 3 was two hundred-thousandths. This phrase has a hyphen in it. The hyphen is an important piece of information that helps us read and write decimals. Let's look at some more examples.

EXAMPLE 5:

Write each phrase as a decimal.

Phrase	Analysis	Fraction	Decimal
three hundred ten thousandths	310 thousandths	$\frac{310}{1,000}$	0.310
three hundred ten-thousandths	300 ten-thousandths	$\frac{300}{10,000}$	0.0300

EXAMPLE 6:

Write each phrase as a decimal.

Phrase	Analysis	Fraction	Decimal
eight hundred thousandths	800 thousandths	$\frac{800}{1,000}$	0.800
eight hundred-thousandths	8 hundred-thousandths	$\frac{8}{100,000}$	0.00008

EXAMPLE 7:

Write each phrase as a decimal.

Phrase	Analysis	Fraction	Decimal
seven hundred millionths	700 millionths	$\frac{700}{1,000,000}$	0.000700
seven hundred-millionths	7 hundred-millionths	$\frac{7}{100,000,000}$	0.00000007

In Examples 5 through 7, we were asked to write phrases as decimals. Some of the words in the phrase indicate the place-value positions, and other words in the phrase indicate the digits to be used. Now let's look at some examples in which we write these kinds of decimals using words.

EXAMPLE 8:

Write each decimal using words.

Decimal	Analysis	Phrase
0.110	110 thousandths	one hundred ten thousandths
0.0100	100 ten-thousandths	one hundred ten-thousandths

EXAMPLE 9:

Write each decimal using words.

Decimal	Analysis	Phrase
0.400	400 thousandths	four hundred thousandths
0.00004	4 hundred-thousandths	four hundred-thousandths

Geometry

Angles

Different Angles have different names:

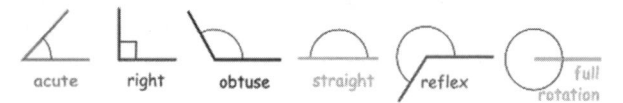

acute right obtuse straight reflex full rotation

An **Acute Angle** is less than 90°.

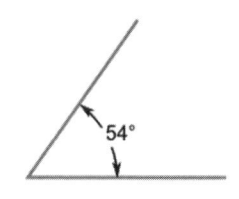

This is an acute angle.

All the angles below are acute angles:

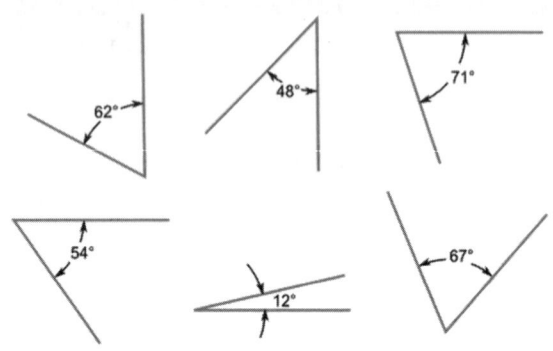

Right Angles

A **right angle** is an internal angle which is equal to 90°.

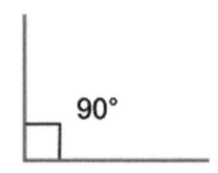

This is a right angle.

Note the special symbol like a box in the angle. If we see this, it is a right angle. The 90° is rarely written in. If we see the box in the corner, we are being told it is a right angle.

All the angles below are right angles:

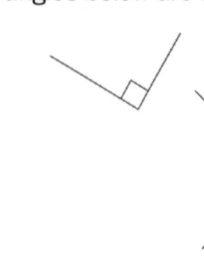

A right angle can be in any orientation or rotation as long as the internal angle is 90°

Obtuse Angles

An **Obtuse Angle** is more than 90° but less than 180°

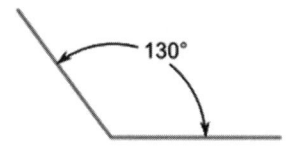

This is an obtuse angle.

All the angles below are obtuse angles:

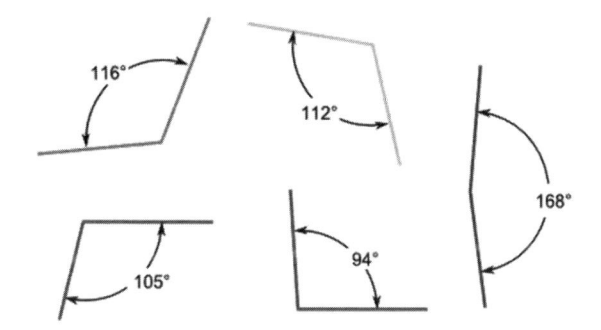

Straight Angle

A **straight angle** is 180°.

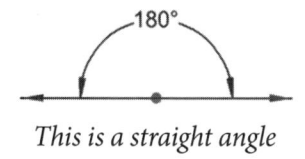

This is a straight angle

A straight angle changes the direction to point the opposite way.

Sometimes people say "You did a complete 180 on that!", meaning you completely changed your mind, idea or direction.

All the angles below are straight angles:

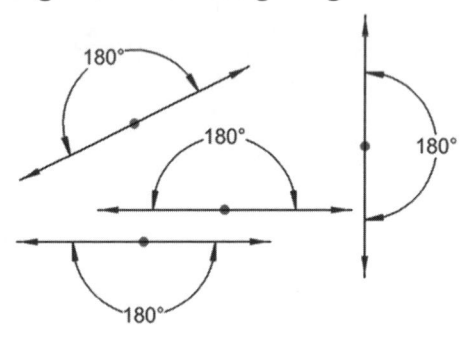

Reflex Angle

A **Reflex Angle** is more than 180° but less than 360°.

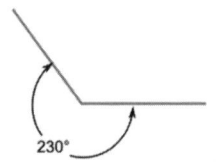

This is a reflex angle

All the angles below are reflex angles:

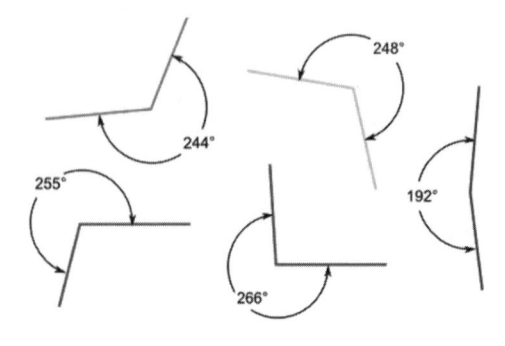

Positive and Negative Angles

When measuring from a line:

- a **positive angle** goes counterclockwise (opposite direction that clocks go)

- a **negative angle** goes clockwise

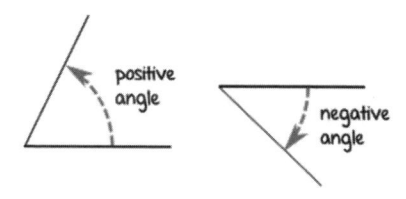

EXAMPLE:

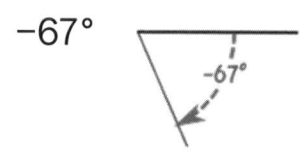

−67°

Parts of an Angle

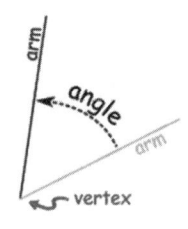

- The corner point of an angle is called the vertex

- The two straight sides are called arms.

- The angle is the amount of turn between each arm.

How to Label Angles

There are two main ways to label angles:

1. give the angle a name, usually a lower-case letter like **a** or **b**, or sometimes a Greek letter like **α** (alpha) or **θ** (theta)

2. or by the three letters on the shape that define the angle, with the middle letter being where the angle actually is (its vertex).

EXAMPLE:

Angle "**a**" is "**BAC**", and angle "**θ**" is "**BCD**"

Algebra

Introduction to Algebra

Algebra is great fun - you get to solve puzzles!

A Puzzle

What is the missing number?

$x - 2 = 4$

OK, the answer is 6, right? Because **6 − 2 = 4.**

Easy stuff.

Well, in Algebra we don't use blank boxes, we use a **letter** (usually an x or y, but any letter is fine). So we write:

$x - 2 = 4$

It is really that simple. The letter (in this case an x) just means "we don't know this yet", and is often called the **unknown** or the **variable**.

And when we solve it we write:

$$x = 6$$

Why Use a Letter?

Because it is easier to write "x" than drawing empty boxes (and easier to say "x" than "the empty box").

If there are several empty boxes (several "unknowns") we can use a different letter for each one.

So x is simply better than having an empty box. We aren't trying to make words with it!

And it doesn't have to be x, it could be y or w, or any letter or symbol we like.

How to Solve

Algebra is just like a puzzle where we start with something like "$x - 2 = 4$" and we want to end up with something like "$x = 6$".

Just remember this

To keep the balance, what we do to **one side** of the "=" we should also do to the **other side**!

Another Puzzle

Solve this one:

$$x + 5 = 12$$

Start with:

$$x + 5 = 12$$

What we are aiming for is an answer like "$x = ...$", and the *plus 5* is in the way of that!

We can cancel out the *plus 5* by doing a *subtract 5* (because 5 − 5 = 0)

So, let us have a go at subtracting 5 from both sides:

$x + 5 - 5 = 12 - 5$

A little arithmetic:

(5 − 5 = 0 and 12 − 5 = 7) becomes: $x + 0 = 7$

Which is just: $x = 7$

SOLVED!

(Quick Check: 7 + 5 = 12)

Common 3D Shapes

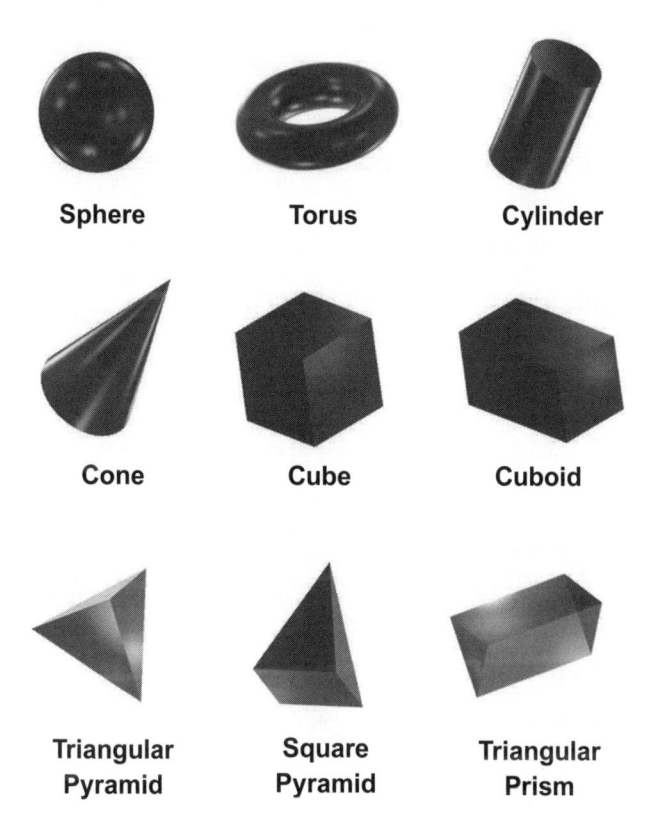

Sphere

Torus

Cylinder

Cone

Cube

Cuboid

Triangular Pyramid

Square Pyramid

Triangular Prism

General Math Terms

A

Absolute value: The magnitude of a number. It is the number with the sign (+ or -) removed and is symbolized using two vertical straight. Also called modulus.

Abstract number: A number with no associated units.

Acute angle: An angle with degree measure less than 90°.

Addition: The process of finding the sum of two numbers, which are called addend and the augend (sometimes both are called the addend).

Algorithm: Any mathematical procedure or instructions involving a set of steps to solve a problem.

Arctan: The inverse of the trigonometric function tangent shown as arctan(x) or $\tan^{-1}(x)$. It is useful in vector conversions and calculations.

Arithmetic mean: $M = (x_1 + x_2 + ... xn) / n$ (n = sample size).

Arithmetic sequence: A sequence of numbers in which each term (subsequent to the first) is generated by adding a fixed constant to its predecessor.

Associative property: A binary operation (*) is defined associative if, for $a*(b*c) = (a*b)*c$. For example, the operations addition and multiplication of natural numbers are associative, but subtraction and division are not.

Asymptote: A straight line that a curve approaches but never meets or crosses. The curve is said to meet the asymptote at infinity. In the equation $y = 1/x$, y becomes infinitely small as x increases but never reaches zero.

Axiom: Any assumption on which a mathematical theory is based.

Average: The sum of several quantities divided by the number of quantities (also called mean).

Avogadro's number: The number of molecules in one mole is called Avogadro's number (approximately 6.022×10^{23} particles/mole).

B

Binary operation: An operation that is performed on just two elements of a set at a time.

Butterfly effect: In a system when a small change results in an unpredictable and disproportionate disturbance, the effect causing this is called a butterfly effect.

C

Calculus: Branch of mathematics concerned with rates of change, gradients of curves, maximum and minimum values of functions, and the calculation of lengths, areas and volumes. It involves determining areas (integration) and tangents (differentiation), which are mutually inverse. Also called real analysis.

Cartesian coordinates: Cartesian coordinates (x,y) specify the position of a point in a plane relative to the horizontal x and the vertical y axes. The x and y axes form the basis of two-dimensional Cartesian coordinate system.

Chaos: Apparent randomness whose origins are entirely deterministic. A state of disorder and irregularity whose evolution in time, though governed by simple exact laws, is highly sensitive to starting conditions: a small variation in these conditions will produce wildly different results, so that long-term behavior of chaotic systems cannot be predicted.

This sensitivity to initial conditions is also known as the butterfly effect (when a **butterfly flaps** its wings in Mexico, the result may be a hurricane in Florida a month later).

Chord: A straight line joining two points on a curve or a circle. See also secant line.

Circle: A circle is defined as the set of points at a given distance (or radius) from its centre. If the coordinates of the centre of a circle on a plane is (a,b) and the radius is r, then $(x-a)^2 + (y-b)^2 = r^2$. The equation that characterises a circle has the same coefficients for x^2 and y^2. The area of a circle is $A = \pi r^2$ and circumference is $C = 2\pi r$. A circle with centre (a,b) and radius r has parametric equations: $x = a + r.\cos\theta$ and $y = b + r.\sin\theta$ ($0 \leq \theta \leq 2\pi$). A 'tangent' is a line, which touches a circle at one point (called the point of tangency) only. A 'normal' is a line, which goes through the centre of a circle and through the point of tangency (the normal is always perpendicular to the tangent). A straight line can be considered a circle; a circle with infinite radius and center at infinity.

Circumference: A line or boundary that forms the perimeter of a circle.

Closure property: If the result of doing an operation on any two elements of a set is always an element of the set, then the set is closed under the operation. For example, the operations addition and multiplication of natural numbers (the set) are closed, but subtraction and division are not.

Coefficient: A number or letter before a variable in an algebraic expression that is used as a multiplier.

Common denominator: A denominator that is common to all the fractions within an equation. The smallest number that is a common multiple of the denominators of two or more fractions is the **lowest** (or least) **common denominator** (LCM).

Common factor: A whole number that divides exactly into two or more given numbers. The largest common factor for two or more numbers is their highest common factor (HCF).

Common logarithm: Logarithm with a base of 10 shown as $\log_{10}$ [$\log_{10} 10^x = x$].

Common ratio: In a geometric sequence, any term divided by the previous one gives the same common ratio.

Commutative property: A binary operation (*) defined on a set has the commutative property if for every two elements, a and b, $a*b = b*a$. For example, the operations addition and multiplication of natural numbers are commutative, but subtraction and division are not.

Complementary angles: Two angles whose sum is 90°. See also supplementary angles.

Complex numbers: A combination of real and imaginary numbers of the form $a + bi$ where a and b are real numbers and i is the square root of -1 (see **imaginary number**). While real numbers can be represented as points on a line, complex numbers can only be located on a plane (See **Types of Numbers**).

Composite number: Any integer which is not a prime number, i.e., evenly divisible by numbers other than 1 and itself.

Congruent: Alike in all relevant respects.

Constant: A quality of a measurement that never changes in magnitude.

Coordinate: A set of numbers that locates the position of a point usually represented by *(x,y)* values.

Cosine law: For any triangle, the side lengths a, b, c and corresponding opposite angles *A, B, C* are related as follows: $a^2 = b^2 + c^2 - 2bc\, cosA$ etc. The law of cosines is useful to determine the unknown data of a triangle if two sides and an angle are known.

Counting number: An element of the set $C = \{1,2,3,...\}$.

Cube root: The factor of a number that, when it is cubed (i.e., x^3) gives that number.

Curve: A line that is continuously bent.

D

Decimal: A fraction having a power of ten as denominator, such as $0.34 = 34/100$ (10^2) or $0.344 = 344/1000$ (10^3). In the continent, a comma is used as the decimal point (between the unit figure and the numerator).

Degree of an angle: A unit of angle equal to one ninetieth of a right angle. Each degree (°) may be further subdivided into 60 parts, called minutes

(60'), and in turn each minute may be subdivided into another 60 parts, called **seconds** (60"). Different types of angles are called acute (<900)< right (900) < obtuse (900-1800) < reflex (1800-3600). See also **radian** (the SI unit of angle).

Denominator: The bottom number in a fraction.

Derivative: The derivative at a point on a curve is the gradient of the tangent to the curve at the given point. More technically, a function ($f'(x_0)$) of a function $y = f(x)$, representing the rate of change of y and the gradient of the graph at the point where $x = x_0$, usually shown as dy/dx. The notation dy/dx suggests the ratio of two numbers dy and dx (denoting infinitesimal changes in y and x), but it is a single number, the limit of a ratio (k/h) as they both approach zero. Differentiation is the process of calculating derivatives..

Differential Equations: Equations containing one or more derivatives (rate of change). As such these equations represent the relationships between the rates of change of continuously varying quantities. The solution contains constant terms (constant of integration) that are not present in the original differential equation. Two general types of differential equations are ordinary differential equations (ODE) and partial differential equations (PDE). When the function involved in the equation depends upon only a single variable, the differential equation is an ODE. If the function depends on several independent variables (so that its derivatives are partial derivatives) then the differential equation is a PDE

Diameter: A straight line that passes from side to side thorough the centre of a circle.

Differential calculus: Differentiation is concerned with rates of change and calculating the gradient at any point from the equation of the curve, $y = f(x)$.

Differential equation: Equations involving total or partial differentiation coefficients and the rate of change; the difference between some quantity now and its value an instant into the future.

Digit: In the decimal system, the numbers 0 through 9.

Dimension: Either the length and/or width of a flat surface (two-dimensional); or the length, width, and/or height of a solid (three-dimensional).

Distributive property: A binary operation (*) is distributive over another binary operation (^) if, $a*(b\char`\^c) = (a*b)\char`\^(a*c)$. For example, the operation of multiplication is distributive over the operations of addition and subtraction in the set of natural numbers.

Division: The operation of ascertaining how many times one number, the **divisor**, is contained in another, the **dividend**. The result is the **quotient**, and any number left over is called the **remainder**. The dividend and divisor are also called the **numerator** and **denominator**, respectively.

Dynamics: The branch of mathematics, which studies the way in which force produces motion.

E

e: Symbol for the base of natural logarithms (2.7182818285...), defined as the limiting value of $(1 + 1/m)^m$.

Equilibrium: The state of balance between opposing forces or effects.

Even number: A natural number that is divisible by two.

Exponent (power, index): A number denoted by a small numeral placed above and to the right of a numerical quantity, which indicates the number of times that quantity is multiplied by itself. In the case of Xn, it is said that X is raised to the power of n. When a and b are non-zero real numbers and p and q are integers, the following rules of power apply:

$a^p \text{x} a^q = a^{p+q}$; $(a^p)^q = a^{pq}$; $(a^{1/n})^m = a^{m/n}$; $a^{1/2} \text{x} b^{1/2} = (ab)^{1/2}$.

Exponential function: A function in the form of $f(x) = a^x$ where x is a real number, and a is positive and not 1. One exponential function is $f(x) = ex$. See **Mathlets: Exponential Functions.**

Extrapolation: Estimating the value of a function or a quantity outside a known range of values. See also interpolation.

F

Factorial: The product of a series of consecutive positive integers from 1 to a given number (n). It is expressed with the symbol (*!*). For example, 5*!* = 5x4x3x2x1 = 120. As a rule ($n!+n$) is evenly divisible by n.

Factor: When two or more natural numbers are multiplied, each of the numbers is a factor of the product. A factor is then a number by which another number is exactly divided (a divisor).

Factorization: Writing a number as the product of its factors which are prime numbers.

Fermat's little theorem: If p is a prime number and b is any whole number, then bp-b is a multiple of p (2^3 - 2 = 6 and is divisible by 3).

Fermat prime: Any prime number in the form of 2^{2n} + 1 (see also **Mersenne prime**).

Fibonacci sequence: Sequence of integers, where each is the sum of the two preceding it. 1,1,2,3,5,8,13,21,... The number of petals of flowers forms a Fibonacci series.

Fractals: Geometrical entities characterised by basic patterns that are repeated at ever decreasing sizes. They are relevant to any system involving self-similarity repeated on diminished scales (such as a fern's structure) as in the study of chaos.

Fraction (quotient): A portion of a whole amount. The term usually applies only to ratios of integers (like 2/3, 5/7). Fractions less than one are called common, proper or vulgar fractions; and those greater than 1 are called improper fraction.

Function (*f*): The mathematical operation that transforms a piece of data into a different one. For example, $f(x) = x^2$ is a function transforming any number to its square.

G

Geometric mean: $G = (x_1.x_2...x_n)^{1/n}$ where n is the sample size. This can also be expressed as antilog ($(1/n)$ S log x). See **Applications of the Geometric Mean; Spizman, 2008: Geometric Mean in Forensic Economy.**

Geometric sequence: A sequence of numbers in which each term subsequent to the first is generated by multiplying its predecessor by a fixed constant (the **common ratio**).

Goldbach conjecture: Every even number greater than 4 is the sum of two odd primes (32 = 13 + 19). Every odd number greater than 7 can be expressed as the sum of three odd prime numbers (11 = 3 + 3 + 5).

Gradient: The slope of a line. The gradient of two points on a line is calculated as rise (vertical increase) divided by run (horizontal increase), therefore, the gradient of a line is equal to the tangent of the angle it makes with the positive x-axis (y/x).

H

Harmonic mean: Of a set of numbers (y_1 to y_i), the harmonic mean is the reciprocal of the arithmetic mean of the reciprocal of the numbers [$H = N / \Sigma (1/y)$]. See also **Wikipedia: Mathematics: Harmonic Mean**. Not to be confused with **Harmonic Ratio**.

Hierarchy of operations: In an equation with multiple operators, operations proceed in the following order: (brackets), exponentiation, division/multiplication, subtraction/summation and from left to right.

Highest common factor (HCF): The greatest natural number, which is a factor of two or more given numbers.

Hypotenuse: The longest side of a right triangle, which lies opposite the vertex of the right angle.

I

***i*:** The square root of -1 (an **imaginary number**).

Identity element: The element of a set which when combined with any element of the same set leaves the other element unchanged (like zero in addition and subtraction, and 1 in multiplication or division).

Imaginary number: The product of a real number x and *i*, where *i*2 + 1 = 0. A complex number in which the real part is zero. In general, imaginary numbers are the square roots of negative numbers.

Improper fraction: A fraction whose numerator is the same as or larger than the denominator; i.e., a fraction equal to or greater than 1.

Infinite: Having no end or limits. Larger than any quantified concept. For many purposes it may be considered as the reciprocal of zero and shown as an 8 lying on its side (∞).

Infinitesimal: A vanishingly small part of a quantity. It equals almost zero.

Integer: Any whole number: positive and negative whole numbers and zero.

Integral calculus: This is the inverse process to differentiation; i.e., a function which has a given derived function. For example, x^2 has derivative 2x, so 2x has x^2 as an integral. A classic application of integral is to calculate areas.

Integration: The process of finding a function given its derived function.

Intersection: The intersection of two sets is the set of elements that are in both sets.

Intercept: A part of a line/plane cut off by another line/plane.

Interpolation: Estimating the value of a function or a quantity from known values on either side of it.

Inverse function: A function which 'does the reverse' of a given function. For example, functions with the prefix arc are inverse trigonometric functions; e.g. arcsin x for the inverse of $\sin(x)$.

Irrational number: A real number that cannot be expressed as the ratio of two integers, and therefore that cannot be written as a decimal that either terminates or repeats. The square root of 2 is an example because if it is expressed as a ratio, it never gives 2 when multiplied by itself. The numbers $e = 3.141592645...$, and $e = 2.7182818...$ are also irrational numbers..

Iteration: Repeatedly performing the same sequence of steps. Simply, solving an algebraic equation with an arbitrary value for the unknown and using the result to solve it again, and again.

L

Least squares method: A method of fitting a straight line or curve based one minimisation of the sum of squared differences (residuals) between the predicted and the observed points. Given the data points (x_i, y_i), it is possible to fit a straight line using a formula, which gives the $y = a + bx$. The gradient of the straight line b is given by $[\Sigma (x_i - m_x)(y_i - m_y)] / [(\Sigma (x - m_x))2]$, where mx and my are the means for xi and yi. The intercept a is obtained by my - bmx.

Linear: A model or function where the input and

output are proportional.

Linear expression: A polynomial expression with the degree of polynomial being 1, i.e., that does not include any terms as the power of a variable. It will be something like, $f(x)=2x^1+3$, but not x^2+2x+4 (the latter is a quadratic expression). Linear equations are closely related to a straight line.

Literal numbers: Letters representing numbers (as in algebraic equations).

Logarithm: The logarithm of a number N to a given base b is the power to which the base must be raised to produce the number N. Written as $\log_b N$. Naturally, $\log_b bx = x$. In any base, the following rules apply: $\log (ab) = \log a + \log b$; $\log (a/b) = \log a - \log b$; $\log (1/a) = -\log a$; $\log a^b = b \log a$; $\log 1 = 0$ and $\log 0$ is undefined.

Lowest common multiple (LCM): The smallest non-zero natural number that is a common multiple of two or more natural numbers (compare with the highest common factor).

M

Matrix: A matrix (plural: matrices) is a rectangular table of data

Mechanics: Study of the forces acting on bodies, whether moving (dynamics) or stationary (statics).

Mersenne prime: A Mersenne number, Mp, has the form 2^p-1, where p is a prime. If M_p itself a prime, then it is called a Mersenne prime. There are 32 such primes known (i.e., not all primes yield a Mersenne prime). (See also **Fermat prime.**)

Mixed number: A number that contains both a whole number and a fraction.

Modulus: The absolute value of a number regardless of its sign, shown as $|x|$ or mod x. For a vector u, the modulus $|u|$ is used to indicate its magnitude calculated using **Pythagoras' theorem:** $|u| = (a^2 + b^2)^{1/2}$.

Multiplication: The process of finding the product of two quantities that are called the multiplicand and the multiplier.

N

Natural logarithm: Logarithm with a base of e, usually abbreviated ln ($ln\ ex = x$).

Natural number: Any element of the set N = {0,1,2,3,...} (positive integers). The inclusion of zero is a matter of definition.

Numerator: The top number in a fraction.

O

Obtuse angle: An angle with a degree measure between 90° and 180°. **See MathWorld: Geometry: Trigonometry: Angles: Obtuse Angle.**

Odd number: A natural number that is not divisible by 2.

Odds: The odds of a success is defined to be the ratio of the probability of a success to the probability of a failure (p/(1-p)).

Ordinate: The vertical coordinate on a plane.

Origin: The point on a graph that represents the point where the x and y axes meet: $(x,y) = (0,0)$.

P

Parallel: Lines or planes that are equidistant from each other and do not intersect.

Perfect number: A number which is equal to the sum of its proper divisors. 6, 28, and 496 are the three of seven known perfect numbers. [6 is a perfect number because its proper divisors (1,2, and 3) total 6.

Permutation: A permutation of a sequence of objects is just a rearrangement of them.

Perpendicular: At right angles to a line or plane.

Pi **(π):** The ratio of the circumference of a circle to its diameter. The value of π is 3.1415926, correct to seven decimal places. The sum of the three angles of a triangle is π radians.

Poisson distribution: The probability distribution of the number of occurrences of random (usually rare and independent) events in an interval or time or space.

Polar equation: A system which describes a point in the plane not by its Cartesian coordinates (x,y) but by its polar coordinates: angular direction (θ) and distance r from the origin (r, θ).

Polygon: A geometric figure that is bound by many straight lines such as triangle, square, pentagon, hexagon, heptagon, octagon etc.

Polynomial: An algebraic expression of the form $a_0 x^n + a_1 x^{n-1} + ... + a_n$, where $a_0, a_1, ..., a_n$ are members of a field (or ring), and n is the degree of the polynomial

Precalculus: A foundational mathematical discipline. Pre-calculus intends to prepare students for the study of calculus. Pre-calculus typically includes a review of algebra, as well as an introduction to exponential, logarithmic and trigonometric functions as preparation for the study of calculus.

Prime factors: Prime factors of a number are a list of prime numbers the product of which is the number concerned. When n=1, for example, $f(x)=2x^1+3$, this is a linear expression. If $n=2$, it is quadratic (for example, $x^2 + 2x + 4$); if $n=3$, it is cubic, if $n=4$, it is quartic and if $n=5$, it is quintic.

Prime number: A natural number other than 1, evenly divisible only by 1 and itself. The numbers 2,3,5,7,11,13,17,19,.... Apart from 2, all primes are odd numbers and odd primes fall into two groups: those that are one less than a multiple of four (3,7,11,19) and those one more than a multiple of four (5,13,17). Every natural number greater than 1 may be resolved into a product of prime numbers; eg 8316 = 22 x 33 x 7 x 11.

Product: The result of a multiplication problem.

Proper divisor: Any number divides another without leaving a remainder.

Proper fraction: A fraction in which the numerator is smaller than the denominator; i.e., a fraction smaller than 1.

Proportion: A type of ratio in which the numerator is included in the denominator. It is the ratio of a part to the whole ($0.0 \leq p \leq 1.0$) that may be expressed as a decimal fraction (0.2), vulgar fraction (1/5) or percentage (20%).

Pythagoras' Theorem: For any right-angled triangle, the square on the hypotenuse equals the sum of the squares on the other two sides.

Q

Quadratic equation: An algebraic equation of the second degree (having one or more variables raised to the second power). The general quadratic equation is $ax^2 + bx + c = 0$, in which a, b, and c are constants (or parameters) and 'a' is not equal to 0.

Quotient (fraction): An algebraic expression in which the numerator is divided by the denominator. Turning a fraction upside down gives the fraction's reciprocal.

R

Radian (rad): The SI unit for measuring an angle formally defined as 'the angle subtended at the centre of a circle by an arc equal in length to the radius of the circle' (the angle of an entire circle is 2π radians; π radians equal 180° (sum of the three angles of a triangle); this is the basis of circumference of a circle formula $2\pi r$). Sum of angles of a triangle equals π radians..

Radius: The distance between the centre of a circle and any point on the circle's circumference.

Rate: The relationship between two measurements of different units such as change in distance with respect to time (miles per hour).

Ratio: The relationship between two numbers or measurements, usually with the same units like the ratio of the width of an object to its length. The ratio a:b is equivalent to the quotient a/b.

Rational number: A number that can be expressed as the ratio of two integers, e.g. 6/7. The set of rational numbers is denotes as 'Q' for quotient..

Real number: Rational (fractions) and irrational (numbers with non-recurring decimal representation) numbers. The set of real numbers is denoted as 'R' for real. In computing, any number with a fractional (or decimal) part. Basically, real numbers are all numbers except imaginary numbers (such as the square root of -1)..

Reciprocal: The multiplicative inverse of a number (i.e., $1/x$). It can be shown with a negative index (x^{-1}).

Reflex angle: An angle with a degree measure between 180 and 360.

Repeating decimal: A decimal that can be written using a horizontal bar to show the repeating digits.

Right angle: An angle with a degree measure 90. An angle which is not an right angle is called oblique angle. See MathWorld: Geometry: Trigonometry: Angles: Right Angle.

Root: If, when a number is raised to the power of n gives the answer a, then this number is the nth root of a ($a^{1/n}$).

Rounding: To give a close approximation of a number by dropping the least significant numbers. For example 15.88 can be rounded up to 15.9 (or 16) and 15.12 can be rounded down to 15.1 (or 15).

S

Scalar: A real number and also a quantity that has magnitude but no direction, such as mass and density.

Scientific notation (exponential notation, standard form): One way of writing very small or very large numbers. In this notation, numbers are shown as $(0<N<10) \times 10^q$. An equivalent form is N.Eq. For example; 365,000 is 3.65×10^5 or 3.65E5.

Secant line: A line that intersects a curve. The intercept is a chord of the curve.

Sequence: An ordered set of numbers derived according to a rule, each member being determined either directly or from the preceding terms.

Sigma (S, s): Represents summation (Σ, σ). See Greek Letters.

Significant figure (s.f.): The specific degree of accuracy denoted by the number of digits used. For example 434.64 has five s.f. but at 3 *s.f.* accuracy it would be shown as '435 (to 3 *s.f.*)'. From the left, the first nonzero digit in a number is the first significant figure, after the first significant number, all digits, including zeros, count as significant numbers (Both 0.3 and 0.0003 have 1 *s.f.*; both 0.0303 and 0.303000 have 3 *s.f.*). If a number has to be reduced to a lower s.f., the usual rounding rules apply (2045.678 becomes 2046 to 4 *s.f.* and 2045.7 to 5 *s.f.*). The final zero even in a whole number is not a s.f. as it only shows the order of magnitude of the number (2343.2 is shown as 2340 to 3 *s.f.*).

Sine law: For any triangle, the side lengths a, b, c and corresponding opposite angles *A, B, C* are related as follows: $\sin A / a = \sin B / b = \sin C / c$. The law of sines is useful for computing the lengths of the unknown sides in a triangle if two angles and one side are known

Skew lines: Two lines in three-dimensional space, which do not lie in the same plane (and do not intersect).

Stationary point: Point at which the derivative of a function is zero. Includes maximum and minimum turning points, but not all stationary points are turning points.

Straight line: A straight line is characterised by an equation ($y = a + bx$), where a is the intercept and b is the gradient/slope. One of the methods for fitting a straight line is the least squares method.

Subtend: To lie opposite and mark out the limits of an angle.

Subtraction: The inverse operation of addition. In the notation $a - b = c$, the terms a, b, and c are called the minuend, subtrahend and difference, respectively.

Supplementary angles: Two angles whose sum is 180°. See also **complementary angles**.

T

Tangent: The tangent of an angle in a right-angled triangle is the ratio of the lengths of the side opposite to the side adjacent [$tan(x) = sin(x) / cos(x)$]. A tangent line is a line, which touches a given curve at a single point. The slope of a tangent line can be approximated by a secant line..

Tangent law: For any triangle, the side lengths a, b, c and corresponding opposite angles A, B, C are related as follows: $(a+b) / (a-b) = \{tan[1/2(A+B)]\} / \{tan[1/2(A-B)]\}$..

Triangle: A three-sided figure that can take several shapes. The three inside angles add up to 180o. Triangles are divided into three basic types: obtuse, right and acute; they are also named by the characteristics of their sides: equilateral, isosceles, and scalene. The area of a triangle is 1/2 x perpendicular height x base.

Trigonometry: The branch of mathematics that is concerned with the trigonometric functions. Trigonometric identities are the results that hold true for all angles.

U

Union: The union of two sets is the set of elements that are in either of the two sets (compare with intersection).

Unit: A standard measurement.

V

Variable: An amount whose value can change.

Vector: A quantity characterized by a magnitude and a direction represented by (1) column form: two numbers (components) in a 2x1 matrix; (2) geometric form: by arrows in the (x,y)-plane; or (3) component form: the Cartesian unit vectors i (x-axis unit vector) and j (y-axis unit vector). The magnitude of a vector $| u |$ is the length of the corresponding arrow and the direction is the angle (θ) the vector makes with the positive x-axis. When a_1 and a_2 are the components of the vector a (magnitude $|a|$ = $(a_1^2 + a_2^2)^{1/2}$), it equals to $a = a_1 i + a_2 j$ in component form, which equals to $a = |a|\cos(\theta)i + |a|\sin(\theta)j$. The angle ($\theta$) can be found as arctan (a_2 / a_1). Cosine rule and sine rule are used for conversion of vectors from one form to another. See Wikipedia: Algebra: Vector, Vector Calculus; Eigenvector.

Vertex: The point where lines intersect.

W

Whole number: Zero or any positive number with no fractional parts.

A SUPER HOMEWORK DICTIONARY FOR PARENTS!

THE **PARENT** COMPANION

CHAPTER 4
SCIENCE

Sci·ence
'sīəns/
noun
noun: **science**

- the intellectual and practical activity encompassing the systematic study of the structure and behavior of the physical and natural world through observation and experiment.

    "the world of science and technology"

    synonyms: branch of knowledge, body of knowledge/information, area of study, discipline, field "the science of criminology"

- a particular area of this.
  plural noun: **sciences**
  "veterinary science"

- a systematically organized body of knowledge on a particular subject.

    "the science of criminology"

Science Giants

Alexander Graham Bell

- **Born:** *March 3, 1847 in Edinburgh, Scotland*
- **Died:** *August 2, 1922 in Nova Scotia, Canada*
- **Best known for:** *Inventing the telephone*

BIOGRAPHY:

Alexander Graham Bell is most famous for his invention of the telephone. He first became interested in the science of sound because both his mother and wife were deaf. His experiments in sound eventually let him to want to send voice signals down a telegraph wire. He was able to get some funding and hire his famous assistant Thomas Watson and together they were able to come up with the telephone. The first words spoken over the telephone were by Alex on March 10, 1876. They were "Mr. Watson, come here, I want to see you". It turns out that other scientists had similar ideas. Bell had to race to the patent office in order to get his patent in first. He was first and, as a result, Bell and his investors had a valuable patent that would change the world. They formed the Bell Telephone Company in 1877. There have been many mergers and name changes over the years, but this company is known today as AT&T.

Where did Alexander Graham Bell grow up?

Bell was born on March 3, 1847 in Edinburgh, Scotland. He grew up in Scotland and was initially homeschooled by his father who was a professor. He later would attend high school as well as the University of Edinburgh.

George Washington Carver

- **Occupation:** *Scientist and educator*
- **Born:** *January 1864 in Diamond Grove, Missouri*
- **Died:** *January 5, 1943 in Tuskegee, Alabama*
- **Best known for:** *Discovering many ways to use the peanut*

BIOGRAPHY:

Where did George grow up?

George was born in 1864 on a small farm in Diamond Grove, Missouri. His mother Mary was a slave owned by Moses and Susan Carver. One night slave raiders came and stole George and Mary from the Carvers. Moses Carver went searching for them, but only found George left by the side of the road.

George was raised by the Carvers. Slavery had been abolished by the 13th amendment and the Carvers had no children of their own. They took care of

George and his brother James like their own children teaching them to read and write.

Growing up George liked to learn about things. He was especially interested in animals and plants. He also liked to read the Bible.

Going to School

George wanted to go to school and learn more. However, there weren't any schools for black children close enough to home for him to attend. George ended up traveling around the midwest in order to go to school. He eventually graduated from high school in Minneapolis, Kansas.

George enjoyed science and art. He initially thought he may want to be an artist. He took some art classes at Simpson College in Iowa where he really enjoyed drawing plants. A teacher of his suggested he combine his love for science, art, and plants and study to become a botanist. A botanist is a scientist that studies plants.

George enrolled in Iowa State to study botany. He was the first African-American student at Iowa State. After earning a bachelor's degree in science, he continued on and earned his master's degree as well. George became known as an expert in botany from the research he conducted at the school.

Professor Carver

After getting his masters, George began to teach as a professor at Iowa State. He was the first African-American professor at the college. However, in 1896 George was contacted by Booker T. Washington.

Booker had opened an all-black college in Tuskegee, Alabama. He wanted George to come teach at his school. George agreed and moved to Tuskegee to head up the agricultural department. He would teach there for the rest of his life.

Crop Rotation

One of the main crops in the south was cotton. However, growing cotton year after year can remove nutrients from the soil. Eventually, the cotton crop will grow weak. Carver taught his students to use crop rotation. One year they would grow cotton, followed by other crops such as sweet potatoes and soybeans. By rotating the crops the soil stayed enriched.

Carver's research and education into crop rotation helped the farmers of the south be more successful. It also helped to diversify the products that they produced.

The Peanut

Another problem for farmers was the boll weevil. This insect would eat cotton and destroy their crops. Carver discovered that boll weevils don't like peanuts. However, farmers weren't so sure that they could make a good living off of peanuts. Carver began to come up with products that could be made from peanuts. He introduced hundreds of new peanut products including cooking oil, dyes for clothing, plastics, fuel for cars, and peanut butter.

George working in his lab

In addition to his work with peanuts, Carver invented products that could be made from other important crops such as the soybean and sweet potato. By making these crops more profitable, farmers could rotate their crops and get more production from their land.

An Expert on Agriculture

Carver became known around the world as an expert on agriculture. He advised President Theodore Roosevelt and the U.S. Congress on matters of agriculture. He even worked with Indian leader Mahatma Gandhi to help with growing crops in India.

Legacy

George Washington Carver was known throughout the south as the "farmer's best friend". His work on crop rotation and innovative products helped many farmers to survive and make a good living. His interest was in science and helping others, not in getting rich. He didn't even patent most of his work because he considered his ideas as gifts from God. He thought they should be free to others.

George died on January 5, 1943 after falling down the stairs at his home. Later, congress would name January 5th as George Washington Carver Day in his honor.

Interesting Facts about George Washington Carver
- *Growing up George had been known as Carver's George. When he started school he went by George Carver. He later added the W in the middle telling his friends it stood for Washington.*

- *People in the south at the time called peanuts "goobers".*

- *Carver would sometimes take his classes out to the farms and teach farmers directly what they could do to improve their crops.*

- *His nickname later in life was the "Wizard of Tuskegee".*

- *He wrote up a pamphlet called "Help for Hard Times" that instructed farmers on what they could do to improve their crops.*

- *It takes over 500 peanuts to make one 12-ounce jar of peanut butter.*

Thomas Edison

- **Occupation:** *Inventor, Businessman*
- **Born:** *February 11, 1847, Milan, OH*
- **Died:** *October 18, 1931, West Orange, NJ*
- **Best known for:** *Invention of the light bulb*

BIOGRAPHY:

Thomas Edison may be the greatest inventor in history. He has over 1000 patents in his name. Many of his inventions still have a major affect on our lives today. He was also a business entrepreneur. Many of his inventions were group efforts in his large invention laboratory where he had many people working for him to help develop, build, and test his inventions. He also started many companies including General Electric, which is one of the biggest corporations in the world today. Where did Edison grow up? Thomas Edison was born in Milan, Ohio on February 11, 1847. His family soon moved to Port Huron, Michigan where he spent most of his childhood. Surprisingly, he did not do well in school and ended up being home schooled by his mother. Thomas was an enterprising young man, selling vegetables, candy and newspapers on trains. One day he saved a child from a runaway train. The child's father repaid Edison by training him as a telegraph operator. As a telegraph operator, Thomas became interested in communications, which would be the focus of many of his inventions. What was Menlo Park? Menlo Park, New Jersey is where Thomas Edison built his research labs. This was the first business or institution with the sole purpose of inventing. They would do research and science and then apply it to practical applications that could be manufactured and built on a large scale. There were a lot of employees working for Edison at Menlo park. These workers were inventors, too, and did a lot of work on Edison's ideas to help turn them into inventions.

What are Thomas Edison's most famous inventions?

Thomas Edison has the patents and credits for many inventions. Three of his most famous include:

The Phonograph

This was the first major invention by Edison and made him famous. It was the first machine that was able to record and playback sound.

Light Bulb

Although he did not invent the first electric light, Edison made the first practical electric light bulb that could be manufactured and used in the home. He also invented other items that were needed make the light bulb practical for use in homes including safety fuses and off/off switches for light sockets.

The Motion Picture

Edison did a lot of work in creating the motion picture camera and helping move forward the progress of practical movies.

Fun Facts About Thomas Edison

- *His middle name was Alva and his family called him Al.*
- *His first two kids had the nicknames Dot and Dash.*
- *He set up his first lab in his parent's basement at the age of 10.*
- *He was partially deaf.*
- *His first invention was an electric vote recorder.*
- *His 1093 patents are the most on record.*
- *He said the words to "Mary had a little lamb" as the first recorded voice on the phonograph.*

Albert Einstein

- **Occupation:** *Scientist and Inventor*
- **Born:** *March 14,1879 Ulm, in Germany*
- **Died:** *18 April 1955 in Princeton, New Jersey*
- **Best known for:** *Theory of Relativity and $E=mc^2$*

BIOGRAPHY:

Albert Einstein was a scientist in the early 1900s. He came up with some of the most important discoveries and theories in all of science. Some people consider him to be one of the smartest people of the 20th century. His face and name are often used as the picture or description of the consummate scientist. Read here to learn more about Albert Einstein; what he was like and what discoveries and inventions he made.

Where did Einstein grow up?

Albert Einstein was born in Ulm, Germany on March 14, 1879. He spent most of his childhood in Munich, Germany. His father had an electronics company and Albert learned a lot about science and electronics from his dad. He really liked math and wanted to pursue math and science in school. He didn't finish school in Germany, but ended up his schooling in Switzerland. Einstein would later move back to Bern, Germany and work in the patent office.

Was Albert Einstein a US citizen?

Albert immigrated to the United States in 1933. He was fleeing from the Nazis in Germany who didn't like Jewish people. If he had stayed in Germany he would not have been able to hold a teaching position at the University as a Jewish person. At one point the Nazis had a bounty on his head. In 1940 Einstein became a US citizen.

$E=mc^2$ and Einstein's Theory of Relativity

Albert Einstein had many discoveries as a scientist, but is most known for his Theory of Relativity. This theory changed much in the way scientists look at the world and set the foundation for many modern inventions, including the nuclear bomb and nuclear energy. One equation from the theory is $E=mc2$. In this formula, "c" is the speed of light and is a constant. It is assumed to be the fastest speed possible in the universe. This formula explains how energy (E) is related to mass (m). The Theory of Relativity explained a lot of how time and distance may change due to the "relative" or different speed of the object and the observer.

What other discoveries is Albert Einstein noted for?

Albert Einstein laid much of the foundation for modern physics.

Some other of his discoveries include:

Photons

In 1905 Einstein came up with the concept that light is made up of particles called photons. Most scientists of his day didn't agree, but later experiments in 1919 showed this to be the case. This became an important discovery for many branches of science and he was awarded the Nobel Prize for Physics in 1921.

Bose-Einstein Condensate

Together with another scientist, Satyendra Bose, Einstien discovered another state of matter. Sort of like liquid or gas or solid states. Today this discovery is used in cool stuff like lasers and superconductors.

Einstein wrote many papers which included theories and models that would help define and move forward our understanding of the world and particularly quantum physics. Some of his work included subjects from a model for a wormhole to the Einstein refrigerator.

The Atomic Bomb

Albert Einstein did not work directly on inventing the Atomic bomb, but his name is closely associated with the bomb. This is because his scientific work and discoveries were key in the bomb's development, specifically his work on energy and mass and his famous equation: $E=mc^2$.

Fun Facts about Albert Einstein

- *Albert experienced speech problems as a child. His parents were worried that he wasn't very smart!*

- *He failed his first try on his entrance exam for college (this gives u all hope!).*

- *He was offered the presidency of Israel.*

- *He auctioned off a hand written version of his Theory of Relativity in 1940 for 6 million dollars in order to help with the war effort.*

- *Albert had a sister named Maja.*

Henry Ford

- **Occupation:** *American Industrialist*
- **Born:** *July 30, 1863, Greenfield Township, MI*
- **Died:** *April 7, 1947, Fair Lane, Dearborn, MI*
- **Best known for:** *Founder of Ford Motor Company*

BIOGRAPHY:

Henry Ford is most famous for starting up the Ford Motor Company. Ford is still one of the world's largest makers of cars including brands such as Ford, Lincoln, Mercury, Volvo, Mazda, and Land Rover. Ford was a pioneer in manufacturing using the assembly line. This enabled his company to manufacture cars on a large scale at a cheap price. For the first time, cars were affordable for the average American family.

Where did Henry Ford grow up?

Henry grew up in Greenfield Township, Michigan. His father was a farmer and wanted Henry to take over the family farm, but Henry had no interest in farming. He was much more interested in machines and building things. He left home at the age of 16 and went to Detroit to become an apprentice machinist. Ford had two brothers and two sisters.

What did Henry Ford invent?

The Assembly Line - It is often stated that Henry Ford invented the assembly line. This is where a large number of products are made one step at a time as they pass down a line. Using an assembly line allows for the mass production of products at a cheaper price than trying to build an entire product one at a time. What Henry Ford did was apply this concept to the automobile and perfect it for the mass production of cars at a much lower price than current production methods. Ford's work in using and streamlining the assembly line was an example of just how powerful an assembly line could be in mass producing products.

The Model T Ford

This was the original car that Henry manufactured using the assembly line process. It was revolutionary in many ways, but primarily in its cost. It was very cheap compared to competitive cars and it was easy to drive and to repair. All this made it perfect for the middle class American. Over 15 million Model T cars were made and, by 1918, over 50% of the cars in America were Model Ts.

Fun facts about Henry Ford

- *Henry worked as an engineer at the Edison Illumination Company where he met Thomas Edison.*

- *His first try at an automobile company was in collaboration with Thomas Edison and was called the Detroit Automobile Company.*

- *Ford had Edison's last breath saved in a test tube and you can still see the test tube at the Henry Ford Museum.*

- *In 1918 he ran for a US Senate seat, but lost.*

- *He was a race car driver early in his career.*

Benjamin Franklin

- **Occupation:** *Statesman and Inventor*
- **Born:** *January 17, 1706 in Boston, Massachusetts*
- **Died:** *April 17, 1790 in Philadelphia, Pennsylvania*
- **Best known for:** *Founding father of the United States*

BIOGRAPHY:

Benjamin Franklin was a modern day Renaissance Man. Like Leonardo da Vinci, Ben Franklin excelled in many areas including science, inventing, politics, writing, music, and diplomacy. He is one of the founding fathers of the United States of America and is often called the "First American".

Where did Ben Franklin grow up?

Ben was born in Boston, Massachusetts on January 17, 1706. His father was a candle maker. Ben stopped going to school when he was 10 and starting working as an apprentice for his brother as printer when he was 12. He gained most of this education by reading a lot of books. Ben ran away when he was 17, breaking his apprenticeship with his brother. He went to Philadelphia, Pennsylvania where he worked as a printer.

What was Franklin's role in the creation of the USA?

Ben first became known to the public as the publisher of the newspaper the Pennsylvania Gazette. He gained some notoriety as an American spokesman when his testimony to the House of Commons in England helped to get the hated Stamp Act repealed.

During the Revolutionary War, Ben Franklin became Pennsylvania's representative to the Second Continental Congress. He was one of the five members that drafted the Declaration of Independence. While Thomas Jefferson was the main author, Ben did make some changes and had an influence on the final draft. One of his key roles in the Revolutionary War was as Ambassador to France. He helped to secure the Treaty of Paris, which got the French army on the side of the Americans and helped to turn the tide of the war. Franklin also took part in the Constitutional Convention and is the only Founding Father to sign all four major documents in the founding of the United States. These include the Declaration of Independence, the Constitution, the Treaty of Paris, and the Treaty of Alliance with France.

What did Benjamin Franklin invent?

As if being a prolific writer and a major player in the founding of the United States wasn't enough, Ben Franklin still found time to be a prominent inventor and scientist.

Perhaps Ben Franklin is most famous for his experiments with electricity. He did many experiments to prove that lightning is in fact electricity. This led to his invention of the lighting rod, which helps to keep buildings safe from lighting.

Other inventions by Ben Franklin include bifocals (a type of glasses), the Franklin stove, an odometer for a carriage, and the glass harmonica. In science he studied and made discoveries in the area of electricity, cooling, meteorology, printing, and the wave theory of light.

Other firsts Ben Franklin was involved in include starting the first public library in America and the first fire department in Pennsylvania.

Fun Facts about Ben Franklin

- *Ben was his dad's 15th child of 17 total children!*
- *While still a teenager he pretended to be Mrs. Silence Dogood and got his letters published in his brother's paper. His brother was not happy when he found out.*
- *Ben Franklin was the first Postmaster General of the United States.*
- *Later in life, Ben set his slaves free and became a fighter for the freedom of slaves.*
- *He didn't patent any of his many inventions, letting people use his ideas for free.*
- *Franklin became fairly wealthy from the publishing of his Poor Richard's Almanac.*

Clouds

Cloud Facts For Kids

- A cloud is a large group of tiny water droplets that we can see in the air.

- Clouds are formed when water on Earth evaporates into the sky and condenses high up in the cooler air. Learn more about the water cycle.

- Rain, snow, sleet and hail falling from clouds is called precipitation.

- Most clouds form in the troposphere (the lowest part of Earth's atmosphere) but occasionally they are observed as high as the stratosphere or mesosphere.

- Clouds can contain millions of tons of water.

- There are a range of different types of clouds, the main types include stratus, cumulus and cirrus.

- Stratus clouds are flat and featureless, appearing as layered sheets.

- Cumulus clouds are puffy, like cotton floating in the sky.

- Cirrus clouds are thin and wispy, appearing high in the sky.

- There are many variations of these 3 main cloud types including stratocumulus, altostratus, altocumulus, cirrostratus and cirrocumulus.

- Fog is stratus type of cloud that appears very close to the ground.

- Clouds can also be made of other chemicals.

- Other planets in our Solar System have clouds. Venus has thick clouds of sulfur-dioxide while Jupiter and Saturn have clouds of ammonia

Dinosaurs

Dinosaur Facts for Kids

Enjoy our fun dinosaur facts for kids and learn about everything from the ferocious Tyrannosaurus Rex to the enormous Diplodocus.

While dinosaurs came a long time before us humans, fossils and modern technology have helped us piece together what dinosaurs may have looked like and even how they might have behaved. Read on for a wide range of cool dinosaur facts that are perfect for kids.

- The word dinosaur comes from the Greek language and means 'terrible lizard'. The word was coined by English paleontologist Richard Owen in 1842 and was meant to refer to Dinosaurs impressive size rather than their scary appearance.

- Dinosaurs ruled the Earth for over 160 million years, from the Triassic period around 230 million years ago through the Jurassic period and until the end of the Cretaceous period around 65 million years ago.

- The time period from 250 million years ago until around 65 million years ago is known as the Mesozoic Era. It is often referred to as the Age of the Dinosaurs because most dinosaurs developed and became extinct during this time.

- It is believed that dinosaurs lived on Earth until around 65 million years ago when a mass extinction occurred.

- Scientists believe that the event leading to the extinction may have been a massive asteroid impact or huge volcanic activity. Events such as these could have blocked out sunlight and significantly changed the Earth's ecology.

- The first dinosaur to be formally named was the Megalosaurus, back in 1824.

- A person who studies dinosaurs is known as a paleontologist.

- Rather than being carnivores (meat eaters), the largest dinosaurs such as the Brachiosaurus and Apatosaurus were actually herbivores (plant eaters).

- To help fight meat eaters such as the Allosaurus or Spinosaurus, many plant eaters had natural weapons at their disposal. Examples of this include the spikes on the tail of the Stegosaurus and the three horns attached to the front of the Triceratops's head shield.

- Pterodactyls are not dinosaurs, they were flying reptiles that lived during the age of dinosaurs but by definition they do not fall into the same category. The same goes for water based reptiles such as Plesiosaurs.

- Birds descended from a type of dinosaurs known as theropods.

- Despite being long extinct, dinosaurs are frequently featured in the media. One of the more memorable examples of this is Michael Crichton's 1990 book Jurassic Park. Adapted to movie in 1993, the story features cloned dinosaurs brought to life with the help of DNA found in mosquitoes trapped in amber.

Rocks

Types of Rocks

Rocks come in many different colors, shapes, and sizes. Because no two rocks are exactly alike, they are a lot of fun to collect. Your rock collection will be truly unique, so start collecting rocks today!

No one else in the world will have a rock collection just like yours. Although, because many rocks have similar properties, we can compare our rocks with those of other collectors if we categorize them into specific types.

The foundation of a great rock collection is to identify your rocks by type.

Geologist classify rocks into three basic groups based on how they were formed in nature.

The types of rocks are:
- Igneous
- Sedimentary
- Metamorphic

To help you identify the types of rocks in your collection, let's look at the characteristics that make up the three types. First, we will look at igneous rocks.

Igneous Rocks

Igneous rocks are formed from melted rock that has cooled and solidified. When rocks are buried deep within the Earth, they melt because of the high pressure and temperature; the molten rock (called magma) can then flow upward or even be erupted from a volcano onto the Earth's surface. When magma cools slowly, usually at depths of thousands of feet, crystals grow from the molten liquid, and a coarse-grained rock forms. When magma cools rapidly, usually at or near the Earth's surface, the crystals are extremely small, and a fine-grained rock results. A wide variety of rocks are formed by different cooling rates and different chemical compositions of the original magma. Obsidian (volcanic glass), granite, basalt, and andesite porphyry are four of the many types of igneous rock. (Credit: U.S. Geological Survey)

Serpentine

A family of silicate minerals rich in magnesium and water, derived from low-temperature alteration or metamorphism of the minerals in ultramafic rocks. Rocks made up of serpentine minerals are called serpentine.

Serpentine minerals are light to dark green, commonly varied in hue, and greasy looking; the mineral feels slippery. (Credit: U.S. Geological Survey)

Metamorphic Rocks

Sometimes sedimentary and igneous rocks are subjected to pressures so intense or heat so high that they are completely changed. They become metamorphic rocks, which form while deeply buried within the Earth's crust. The process of metamorphism does not melt the rocks, but instead transforms them into denser, more compact rocks. New minerals are created either by rearrangement of mineral components or by reactions with fluids that enter the rocks. Some kinds of metamorphic rocks-- granite gneiss and biotite schist are two examples-- are strongly banded or foliated. (Foliated means the parallel arrangement of certain mineral grains that gives the rock a striped appearance.)

Anyone who wishes to collect rocks should become familiar with the characteristics of these three rock groups. Knowing how a geologist classifies rocks is important if you want to transform a random group of rock specimens into a true collection. (Credit: U.S. Geological Survey)

Ice Age

What is an ice age?

An ice age is a period in Earth's history when the ice on the polar caps significantly expanded due to an overall lowering of the Earth's global temperatures. During these periods land in North America and Northern Europe were covered by giant ice fields and glaciers.

How do scientists know about ice ages?

Scientists have figured out when past ice ages likely occurred by studying the geology of the land. There are many geological features in Northern Europe and North America that can only be explained by the movements of giant glaciers. Scientists also study the chemicals in rocks and fossil evidence to determine when ice ages have occurred.

Are we living in an ice age?

Yes, you may be surprised to know that we are currently living in an ice age called the Quaternary ice age. The Earth is in a warmer stage of the ice age called an interglacial period.

Glacial and Interglacial Periods

There are periods within ice ages that scientists define as glacial and interglacial.

- **Glacial:** A glacial period is a cold period when the glaciers are expanding.
- **Interglacial:** An interglacial period is a warm period where the glaciers may be receding.

Five Major Ice Ages

Over the course of millions of years, scientists believe that the Earth has experienced at least five major ice ages.

- **Huronian:** The Huronian ice age was one of the longest ice ages in the Earth's history. It lasted from about 2400 to 2100 million years ago. Scientists think it may have been caused by a lack of volcanic activity lowering the carbon dioxide in the atmosphere.

- **Cryogenian:** The Cryogenian ice age occurred from 850 to 635 million years ago. It is possible that ice sheets reached all the way to the equator. Scientists sometimes call this a "Snowball Earth."

- **Andean-Saharan:** The Andean-Saharan ice age occurred between 460 to 430 million years ago.

- **Karoo:** The Karoo ice age lasted around 100 million years between 360 to 260 million years ago. It is named after glacial tills in Karoo, South Africa that scientists think were developed during this ice age.

- **Quaternary:** The most recent ice age is the Quaternary ice age. By scientific definition, we are currently in an interglacial stage of this ice age. It started around 2.5 million years ago and is still going.

What can cause an ice age?

The Earth is constantly undergoing changes. These changes can impact the global climate.

Some of the changes that can influence an ice age include:

- **Earth's orbit:** Changes in the Earth's orbit (called Milankovitch cycles) can cause the Earth to be closer to the Sun (warmer) or further from the sun (colder). Ice ages can occur when we are further from the Sun.
- **Sun:** The amount of energy output by the Sun also changes. Low cycles of energy output can help in producing an ice age.
- **Atmosphere:** Low levels of greenhouse gasses such as carbon dioxide can cause the Earth to cool leading to an ice age.
- **Ocean currents:** Ocean currents can have a great impact on the Earth's climate. Changes in currents can cause ice sheets to build up.
- **Volcanoes:** Volcanic activity can introduce huge amounts of carbon dioxide into the atmosphere. The lack of volcanoes can cause an ice age. Increased volcanic activity can put an end to an ice age as well.

Interesting Facts about Ice Ages

- *The current interglacial period that the Earth is in is called the Holocene period.*
- *Most of Canada was covered with ice just 20,000 years ago.*
- *An ice age can occur if the global temperature drops just a few degrees for a long period of time.*
- *Ice and snow can reflect the Sun's rays and energy, further lowering the temperature and increasing the length of an ice age.*
- *Mammals from the last ice age that are now extinct include the wooly mammoth and the saber-toothed cat.*

Weather

Climate

The average weather conditions in a particular location or region at a particular time of the year. Climate is usually measured over a period of 30 years or more

Climate change

A significant change in the Earth's climate. The Earth is currently getting warmer because people are adding heat-trapping greenhouse gases to the atmosphere. The term "global warming" refers to warmer temperatures, while "climate change" refers to the broader set of changes that go along with warmer temperatures, including changes in weather patterns, the oceans, ice and snow, and ecosystems around the world.

Global warming

An increase in temperature near the surface of the Earth. Global warming has occurred in the distant past as the result of natural causes. However, the term is most often used to refer to recent and ongoing warming caused by people's activities. Global warming leads to a bigger set of changes referred to as global climate change.

Weather

The condition of the atmosphere at a particular place and time. Some familiar characteristics of the weather include wind, temperature, humidity, atmospheric pressure, cloudiness, and precipitation. Weather can change from hour to hour, day to day, and season to season.

Glossary of Scientific Terms

A

Absolute zero: The lowest theoretical temperature (0K = -273.16°C) where all molecular activity ceases.

Acceleration: Rate of change of velocity.

Acid: A compound that yields hydrogen ions (H+) when in aqueous solution. Acids have a sour taste and turn blue litmus red.

Activation energy: The energy required to initiate a chemical reaction.

Adiabatic system: A system that neither gains or looses heat.

Alcohol: Organic compound used in gums, resins, dyes and perfumes. Fermentation produces ethanol not alcohol.

Alkali: A base that is soluble in water.

Allele: Gene variant.

allotrope: Element with more than one natural form.

Alloy: A substance formed by the combination of two or more elements, at least one of which must be a metal.

Amino acids: Carbon, hydrogen, oxygen and nitrogen compounds the composition of which are determined by genes.

Anion: A negative ion.

Atomic number: The number of protons in an atom.

Atomic symbol: The letters representing each of the elements.

Atomic weight: The average weight of an atom.

Atoms: Composite particles of protons, neutrons and electrons. The smallest part of a substance that can take part in a chemical reaction. Click here for more information.

B

Baryon: A three quark hadron. The most common baryons are protons and neutrons.

Base: A compound that yields hydroxide (OH-) ions when in aqueous solution. Bases have a bitter taste, feel greasy and turn red litmus blue.

Biosynthesis: The production of cellular material.

Boiling point: The temperature at which a liquid turns to a vapour.

Bond: A chemical link between atoms.

C

Capacitance: The ability to store an electric charge.

Carbohydrates: The major energy source within plants and animals: sugars, starches and glucose polymers.

Carbon: The basic element in all organic compounds.

Catalyst: A substance that reduces the activation energy of a reaction.

Cation: A positive ion.

Cell: The smallest independent part of an organism.

Chain reaction: Polymerisation initiated by the bonding of a free radical with a monomer.

Charge: The amount of unbalanced electricity in a system. Either positive or negative.

Chemical Equation: The mathematical representation of a chemical reaction.

Chemical (empirical) Formula: The ratio of elements in a substance. For example: the chemical formula of common salt is NaCl, sodium and chlorine in a ratio of 1:1.

Chemical Reaction: The transformation of substances by the rearrangement of their atoms.

Chromosomes: DNAmolecules that contain the set of instructions required to build and maintain cells.

Compound: A substance containing more than one element.

Conduction: Heat or electricity transfer through molecular interaction, eg: heat passing along a metal bar.

Convection: Heat transfer through the movement of a fluid, eg: warm air rising.

Coulomb Attraction: Electrostatic attraction between bodies of opposite charge

Covalent Bond: A bond formed between atoms that share electrons.

Crystal: Solid substance with a regular geometirc arrangement of atoms.

Cytosol: Jelly-like substance within cells.

D

Density: The mass per unit volume in a substance.

Diffraction: The deviation in the path of a wave that encounters the edge of an obstacle.

Diffusion: The random movement of molecules within a fluid.

DNA: Deoxyribonucleic acid: Twisted helical polymer chains. See chromosomes.

E

Elasticity: The ability of a body to regain its original shape after deformation.

Electric current: A flow of electrons through a conductor, the size of the current is proportional to the rate of electron flow.

Electrons: Negatively charged atomic particles.

Electromagnetic waves: Waves with both an electric and magnetic component. They are: radio, micro, infra-red, visible light, ultraviolet, X and gamma rays.

Electrolyte: An ion solution that is an electrical conductior.

Element: A substance composed of atoms all with the same atomic number. A substance that cannot be split chemically into smaller substances.

Endothermic reaction: A reaction in which heat is absorbed ie: melting or boiling.

Energy: The capacity to do work. Work is done by transferring energy from one form to another. For example the chemical energy in a fuel is converted to thermal energy as it burns. See also Laws of Thermodynamics.

Entropy: The state of disorder in a thermodynamic system: the more energy the higher the entropy.

Enzymes: Biological catalysts, proteins that control specific processes within the body.

Equilibrium: A stable situation in which products and reactants are balanced.

Evaporation: The change of state of a substance from a liquid to a gas below its boiling point.

Evolution: Natural selection, the survival of the fittest, is the driving force behind evolution and is measured by a species viability and fecundity. Governed by Darwin's theory of evolution by natural selection:

1. The distinguishing features (characters) of an organism may affect it fitness.
2. The design of an species (its morphology) differs within a population and may improve its fitness.
3. An organism may be susceptible to a lack of vital resources, predation and disease reducing its fitness.
4. The characters that improve fitness must be inherited. Individuals that inherit these characters will survive at the expense of those who do not.
5. Mutation is essential for evolution: the inheritance of non-standard genes that improve fitness.

Note: *Fitness is the ability to survive and reproduce, not necessarily a measure of physical fitness.*

Exothermic Reaction: A reaction from which heat is lost eg: combustion.

F

Fats: Molecules of fatty acids or glycerol. Used as a food store, insulation and for shock absorption.

Fecundity: The ability to breed.

Field: A region in space that is defined by a vector function. Common fields are: gravitational, electric and magnetic.

Fission: Splitting the nucleus of an atom into smaller units.

Fluid: A liquid or gas.

Force: An action (transfer of energy) that will accelerate a body in the direction of the applied force. See Newtons Laws of Motion.

Free radical: A highly reactive molecule used to start the production of a polymer chain.

Frequency: The rate as which periodic motion repeats itself.

Friction: The interaction between surfaces: a measure of the resistance felt when sliding one body over another.

Fundamental Particles: Those particles that are not known to contain any smaller components: leptons, quarks and gauge bosons.

Fusion:
1. Change of state of a substance from a solid to a liquid.
2. The joining together of two atomic nuclei.

G

Gametes: Sex cells (spermatozoa or ova) that carry the genes donated by each parent.

Gauge bosons: Particles that mediate the transfer of energy between other particles: protons, gravitons, W and Z particles.

Gene: A unit of inheritance. A section of DNA comprising a sequence of four bases: adenine, guanine, cytosine and thymine.

Genome: The collective noun for a set of genes. The human genome contains 100 000 genes.

Gravity: The attraction that all bodies have for one another.

H

Hadrons: Quark composites: mesons and baryons. Protons and neutrons are the most common hadrons.

Half-life: The time taken for the level of radioactivity in an element to halve.

Halogen: Highly reactive gases forming group 7 of the periodic table.

Heat: The internal energy of a body (substance).

Hydrocarbon: Compounds containing only hydrogen and carbon atoms.

ideal gas. One which obeys the ideal gas law. At low pressures, real gases behave like ideas gases.

I

Inertia: Tendency of a body to remain at rest or move in straight line.

Inheritance: The features of an organism are determined by a set of chromosomes. These originate in the parents and are passed on to an offspring during fertilisation. It follows then that since chromosomes are inherited, all the features of an organism must be inherited.

Ion: Atom with an unbalanced electrical charge caused by the loss or gain of one or more electrons.

Ionic Bond: An bond formed by the electro-magnetic attraction between ions of opposite charge.

Isomer: Chemical compounds with the same composition but different shapes.

Isomeric Structure: The shape of a molecule. The isomeric structure is determined by the order in which the atoms are bonded together.

Isotope: An element that has more or less neutrons than normal. Many isotopes are radioactive.

K

Kinetic Energy: The energy possessed by a body in motion.

L

Latent heat: The amount of energy required to change a solid to a liquid or liquid to a gas.

Laws of Themodynamics:

1. The amount of energy in the universe is fixed. It cannot be created or destroyed only changed from one state to another.
2. Heat cannot pass from a cold to a hot body. The opposite condition where heat always flows from a hot to a cold body is valid for the whole universe.

Lens: Light modifier. Convex lenses focus and concave lens diffuse light waves.

Leptons: Fundamental particles that are relatively non-reactive and capable of an independent existence: electrons, muons, tau particles and neutrinos.

Light: The visible part of the electromagnetic spectrum: red, orange, yellow, green, blue, indigo and violet. White light is a combination of all the above colours.

M

Magnet: A body which produces a magnetic field. All magnets are di-pole and follow the rule that like poles repel and unlike poles attract.

Mass: The quantity of matter in a body.

Mesons: Two quarkhadrons, the product of radioactive decay.

Metals: Elements characterised by their opacity, malleability and thermal and electrical conductivity.

Mitochondria: Organelles that convert glucose into energy.

Molecular formula: The number and types of atom in a molecule. For example the molecular formula of methane is CH4, one atom of carbon and four atoms of hydrogen.

Molecule: A group of atoms bonded together. It is the smallest part of a substance that retains the chemical properties of the whole.

Moment: A rotating effect. See torque.

Momentum: The product of mass times velocity. Momentum is conserved in any system of particles.

Monomers: Small molecules that link together to form a polymer.

N

Neutralization: A reaction in which the characteristics of an acid or base disappear.

Neutrons: Particles with zero charge forming part of an atomic nuclei. 3 quarkhadrons.

Newtons Laws of Motion: Classical laws which enable the prediction of the path of any object from a grain of sand to entire galaxies:

1. A body will remain at rest or move with a constant velocity unless acted upon by an outside force.

2. The acceleration of a body is proportional to the applied force. This is expressed by the universal formula: Force = mass × acceleration.

3. For every action there is an equal and opposite reaction.

Noble gases: Elements with zero valency. They form group 0 in the periodic table and are non-reactive.

Nucleus:
1. Organelle containing the chromosomes.
2. That part of an atom containing the protons and neutrons.

O

Organelles: Specialized organs within cells.

Organic compounds: Substances that contain carbon.

Ozone: An isotope of oxygen that blocks ultra-violet radiation. Normally found in the stratosphere.

P

pH Scale: The strength of acids and bases. Pure water has a pH value of 7, acids have a lower value and bases higher.

Phase changes: Freezing or boiling.

Photo-synthesis: The conversion of water and carbon-dioxide by plants into glucose and oxygen. Light is used as an energy source.

Photons: Fundamental quantum particles. It is the interaction of photons with other particles that drives the universe.

Polymerisation: The repetitive bonding of small molecules (monomers) to produce large molecules (polymers).

Polymers: Long chain molecules such as PVC, nylon

or DNA produced by the polymerisation of monomers.

Potential difference: The voltage difference between two points. Electricity flows from a high to low level of potential.

Potential energy: Amount of useable energy within a body at rest.

Power: Amount of work done per second.

Products: The substances produced in a chemical reaction.

Proteins: Amino acid polymers with specific biological functions, especially the growth, regeneration and repair of cells.

Protons: Positively charged particles forming part of atomic nuclei. 3 quark hadrons.

Q

Quantum theory: The theory that energy can only be absorbed or radiated in discrete values or quanta. All particles are subject to quantum theory. Click here to find out more.

Quarks: Fundamental particles, incapable of independent existence, that combine to form particles such as protons and neutrons.

R

Radiation:

1. Transfer of heat between bodies without a change in the temperature of the intervening medium.

2. Any release of energy from its source.

Radioactivity: The spontaneous release of energy from atomic nuclei.

Reactants: The substances that take part in a chemical reaction.

Refraction: The deflection of a wave as it passes from one medium to another, eg through a lens.

Relative atomic mass (RAM): The mass of an atom relative to one atom of carbon. Carbon has a RAM of 12.

Relativity: The relative values of time, motion, mass and energy of a body in motion. Click here for more information

Reproduction: Reproduction is the process by which a new organism is produced. The first stage in the production of any organism is the fertilization of an ova by spermatozoa (or spores on the case of plants). Fertilization produces a single cell called a zygote, which contains all the information required to build the adult organism. The progression (growth) from zygote to adult is achieved through cell division.

Resistance: Opposition to current flow in a conductor.

Resonance: A state where the natural frequency of a body equals an applied frequency.

Respiration: The production of energy by the oxidization of glucose.

S

Scalar: A quantity that is defined by its magnitude only (ie energy, temperature).

Simple Harmonic Motion: A repeating motion about a central equilibrium point (pendulum, weighted spring).

Special Relativity: The observable effects on a body in motion. As velocity increases, time slows down, mass increases and lengths contract.

Speciation: A group of organisms that are able to interbreed all belong to the same species. It follows then that organisms that are unable to interbreed belong to separate species.

Specific Heat: The heat capacity of a body.

Standard model: The organization and relationships between fundamental particles. Click here for more information.

Strain: The deformation of a body under an applied load.

Stress: The measure of the force acting on a body.

T

Temperature: How hot one body is when compared to another.

Torque: The tendency of a body to rotate under an applied force.

U

Uncertainty: It is impossible to know exactly where something is and where it is going. This is a fundamental law of nature has a major effect on quantum theory.

V

Valency: A measure of the reactivity of an element.

Vector: A quantity that is determined by its magnitude and direction: forces and fields (see scalar).

Velocity: The rate of change of distance with respect to time.

Viability: The ability to survive to adulthood.

Viscosity: The internal friction of a fluid, thick fluids have a high viscosity and thin fluids low.

W

Water Cycle: The water cycle starts with evaporation, then condensation, to precipitation, and finally runoff.

Weather Forecasting: Forecasting weather (meteorology) is a major part of today's world. The task of predicting is the primary objective of the science of meteorology.

Weathering: The breakdown of rock that takes place near the surface of earth.

Weight: The gravitational force exerted on a mass.

Work: The amount of energy transferred to a system.

Z

Zygote: A fertilised egg, the fusion of a male and female gamete.

A SUPER HOMEWORK DICTIONARY FOR PARENTS!

CHAPTER 5
SOCIAL **STUDIES**

so·cial stud·ies
ˈsīəns/
noun
plural noun: **social studies**

- various aspects or branches of the study of human society, considered as an educational discipline.

U.S. Constitutional Amendments

Amendment: a written change to the Constitution

Bill of Rights: The first ten amendments to become apart of the U.S. Constitution in 1791.

Amendment #1
Freedom of religion, speech, press, assembly, and petition

Amendment #2
Right to bear arms

Amendment #3
No one may be forced to house soldiers

Amendment #4
Protects against unreasonable search and seizure

Amendment #5
Rights of the criminally accused (indictment by grand jury, no double jeopardy, no self incrimination, due process of the law, eminent domain)

Amendment #6
Rights to a speedy trial by jury (speedy trial, impartial jury, informed of charges, right to an attorney)

Amendment #7
Rights to a jury trial in CIVIL CASES, more than $20 - people sue over money/property

Amendment #8
No excessive bail, no cruel and unusual punishment

Amendment #9
People have other basic rights not listed in Constitution

Amendment #10
All powers not given to the federal government are left for the states to take care of/decide

Amendment #11
Federal courts do not have jurisdiction in cases against a state

Amendment #12
Provides for separate elections for president and vice president

Amendment #13
Abolishes slavery

Amendment #14
Provides equality for all citizens; state governments must follow previously passed amendments

Amendment #15
All males have the right to vote

Amendment #16
Congress has the power to pass direct taxes, such as income tax

Amendment #17
Senators are to be elected by the voters in their state; governor fills state senator positions if position opens during a term

Amendment #18
Selling and drinking of alcoholic beverages is made illegal (prohibited)

Amendment #19
Gives women the right to vote

Amendment #20
Beginning of President, VP and Congress terms in office begins in January; presidential succession can take place before Presidential inauguration

Amendment #21
Selling and drinking of alcoholic beverages is made legal (allowed again, #18 was repealed or cancelled by this amendment)

Amendment #22
Presidents may serve no more than 2 terms or a total of 10 years

Amendment #23
District of Columbia is allowed presidential Electoral College votes

Amendment #24
Eliminates poll tax (no required payment needed to vote)

Amendment #25
Provides for presidential succession and filling a vacant office of vice president, if VP dies or his removed from office

Amendment #26
Lowers voting age from 21 to 18

Amendment #27
Congressional compensation increases may not take effect until after that congressional term is over (their pay raise doesn't go into effect until new term)

States and Capitals

Alabama	Montgomery
Alaska	Juneau
Arizona	Phoenix
Arkansas	Little Rock
California	Sacramento
Colorado	Denver
Connecticut	Hartford
Delaware	Dover
Florida	Tallahassee
Georgia	Atlanta
Hawaii	Honolulu
Idaho	Boise
Illinois	Springfield
Indiana	Indianapolis
Iowa	Des Moines

Kansas	Topeka
Kentucky	Frankfort
Louisiana	Baton Rouge
Maine	Augusta
Maryland	Annapolis
Massachusetts	Boston
Michigan	Lansing
Minnesota	St. Paul
Mississippi	Jackson
Missouri	Jefferson City
Montana	Helena
Nebraska	Lincoln
Nevada	Carson City
New Hampshire	Concord
New Jersey	Trenton
New Mexico	Santa Fe
New York	Albany
North Carolina	Raleigh
North Dakota	Bismarck
Ohio	Columbus
Oklahoma	Oklahoma City
Oregon	Salem
Pennsylvania	Harrisburg
Rhode Island	Providence
South Carolina	Columbia
South Dakota	Pierre
Tennessee	Nashville

Texas	Austin
Utah	Salt Lake City
Vermont.	Montpelier
Virginia	Richmond
Washington.	Olympia
West Virginia.	Charleston
Wisconsin	Madison
Wyoming.	Cheyenne

Civil Rights Leaders

Civil rights leaders are influential figures in the promotion and implementation of political freedom and the expansion of personal civil liberties and rights. They work to protect individuals and groups from political repression and discrimination by governments and private organizations, and seek to ensure the ability of all members of society to participate in the civil and political life of the state.

Civil rights include individual rights to equal protection and service, privacy, freedom of thought, freedom of expression, freedom of speech, freedom of assembly, freedom to travel, freedom of worship, protection of civil liberties, the right to vote, and the right to freely share ideas and opinions through all forms of communication and media. People who motivated themselves and then led others to gain and protect these rights and liberties include:

Ralph Abernathy *(1926–1990)*
American activist, Southern Christian Leadership Conference (SCLC) official

B.R. Ambedkar *(1891–1956)*
Indian activist for caste abolition, writer, philosopher, economist, co-wrote and influenced Indian constitution which focused on social rights.

Susan B. Anthony *(1820–1906)*
American Women's suffrage leader, speaker, inspiration

Ella Baker *(1903–1986)*
American SCLC activist, initiated the Student Nonviolent Coordinating Committee (SNCC)

James Baldwin *(1924–1987)*
American essayist, novelist, public speaker, SNCC activist

Daisy Bates *(1914–1999)*
American organizer of the Little Rock Nine school desegregation events.

Dana Beal *(1947–)*
American pro-hemp activist, organizer, speaker, initiator.

Jeremy Bentham *(1748-1832)*
British philosopher, writer, and teacher on civil rights, inspiration.

James Bevel *(1936–2008)*
American organizer and Direct Action leader, SCLC's main strategist, movement initiator, and movement director.

Claude Black *(1916–2009)*
American civil rights movement activist

Antoinette Brown Blackwell *(1825-1921)*
founded American Woman Suffrage Association with Lucy Stone in 1869.

Julian Bond *(1940–)*
American activist, politician, scholar, lawyer, NAACP chairman.

Lenny Bruce *(1925-1966)*
American free speech advocate, comedian, political satirist.

Lucy Burns *(1879–1966)*
American women's suffrage/voting rights leader.

Stokely Carmichael *(1941–1998)*
American SNCC and Black Panther activist, organizer, speaker.

Carrie Chapman Catt *(1859–1947)*
suffrage leader, president National American Woman Suffrage Association, founder League of Women Voters and International Alliance of Women.

Cesar Chavez *(1927–1993)*
Chicano activist, organizer, trade unionist, inspiration.

Claudette Colvin *(1939–)*
American Montgomery Bus Boycott pioneer, independent activist.

Marvel Cooke *(1903–2000)*
American journalist, writer, trade unionist.

Humberto "Bert" Corona *(1918–2001)*
labor and civil rights leader.

Dorothy Cotton *(1930–)*
American SCLC official, activist, organizer, and leader.

Eugene Debs *(1855–1926)*
American organizer, campaigner for the poor, women, dissenters, prisoners.

Andre DiMino *(1950–)*
Italian-American civil rights activist.

Frederick Douglass *(1818–1895)*
American abolitionist, women's rights and suffrage advocate, writer, organizer, black rights activist, inspiration.

W. E. B. Du Bois *(1868–1963)*
American writer, scholar, founder of NAACP.

Charles Evers *(1922–)*
American civil rights movement activist.

Medgar Evers *(1925–1963)*
American, NAACP official in the Mississippi Movement.

James Farmer *(1920–1999)*
Congress of Racial Equality (CORE) leader and activist.

James Forman *(1928–2005)*
American SNCC official and civil rights movement activist.

Marie Foster *(1917–2003)*
American voting rights activist, a local leader in the Selma Voting Rights Movement.

Frankie Muse Freeman *(1916–)*
American civil rights attorney, and the first woman to be appointed to the United States Commission on Civil Rights.

Golden Frinks *(1920-2004)*
American civil rights organizer in North Carolina and field secretary of the Southern Christian Leadership Conference.

Betty Friedan *(1921–2006)*
American writer, women's rights activist, feminist.

Kasturba Gandhi *(1869–1944)*
wife of Mohandas Gandhi, activist in South Africa and India, often led her husband's movements in India when he was imprisoned.

Mohandas Gandhi *(1869–1948)*
Indian activist, movement leader, writer, philosopher, and teacher.

William Lloyd Garrison *(1805–1879)*
writer, organizer, feminist, initiator.

Dick Gregory *(1932–)*
American free speech advocate and activist in the civil rights movement, comedian.

Olympe de Gouges *(1748–1793)*
French women's rights pioneer, writer, beheaded during French Revolution.

Prathia Hall *(1940–2002)*
American SNCC activist, a leading speaker in the civil rights movement.

Fred Hampton *(1948–1969)*
American NAACP youth leader and Black Panther activist, organizer, speaker.

Fannie Lou Hamer *(1917–1977)*
activist in Mississippi movements

Harry Hay *(1912–2002)*
early leader in American LGBT rights movement, founder Mattachine Society

Lola Hendricks *(1932–)*
activist, local leader in Birmingham Movement

Jack Herer *(1939–2010)*
American pro-hemp activist, speaker, organizer, author

Gordon Hirabayashi *(1918–2012)*
Japanese-American civil rights hero

Myles Horton *(1905–1990)*
American teacher of nonviolence, pioneer activist, founded and led the Highlander Folk School

T.R.M. Howard *(1908–1976)*
founder of Mississippi's Regional Council of Negro Leadership

Julia Ward Howe *(1818–1910)*
American writer, organizer, suffragette

Dolores Huerta *(1930–)*
American labor and civil rights activist, initiator, organizer

John Peters Humphrey *(1905–1995)*
author of Universal Declaration of Human Rights

Harish Iyer *(1979–)*
Indian gender and sexuality rights activist, campaigns against child sexual abuse and for animal rights, inspiration.

Jesse Jackson *(1941–)*
American civil rights activist, politician

Nellie Stone Johnson *(1905–2002)*
labor and civil rights activist

Toyohiko Kagawa *(1888–1960)*
Japanese labour activist, Christian reformer, author

Meir Kahane *(1932-1990)*
controversial Jewish rights leader, founder of the Jewish Defense League

Ashok Row Kavi *(1947–)*
Indian LGBT rights activist, pioneer Indian gay rights movement, founder of Humsafar Trust

Abby Kelley *(1811–1887)*
American abolitionist and suffragette

Coretta Scott King *(1927–2006)*
American SCLC leader, activist, inspiration

Martin Luther King, Jr. *(1929–1968)*
SCLC co-founder/president/chairman, activist, author, speaker, inspiration

James Lawson *(1928–)*
American minister and activist, SCLC's teacher of nonviolence in late 1950s and early 1960s civil rights movement

Bernard Lafayette *(1940–)*
American SCLC and SNCC activist, organizer, and leader

John Lewis *(1940–)*
American Nashville Student Movement and SNCC activist, organizer, speaker, inspiration

Sigmund Livingston *(1872-1946)*
Jewish rights activist, founder of the Anti-Defamation League

Joseph Lowery *(1921–)*
American SCLC leader and co-founder, activist

Clara Luper *(1923–2011)*
American sit-in movement leader in Oklahoma, activist

James Madison *(1751–1836)*
American founding father, introduced and lobbied for the U.S. Bill of Rights

Nelson Mandela *(1918–2013)*
South African statesman, leading figure in anti-apartheid movement, inspiration

George Mason *(1725–1792)*
American who wrote the Virginia Declaration of Rights and influenced U.S. Bill of Rights

Rigoberta Menchú *(1959–)*
Guatemalan indigenous rights leader, co-founder Nobel Women's Initiative

James Meredith *(1933–)*
American independent student leader and self-starting Mississippi activist

Mamie Till Bradley Mobley *(1921-2003)*
American who held an open casket funeral for her son, Emmett Till; speaker, activist

Charles Morgan, Jr. *(1930–2009)*
American attorney, established principle of "one man, one vote"

Harvey Milk *(1930–1978)*
American politician, gay rights activist and leader, inspiration

Bob Moses *(1935–)*
leader, activist, and organizer in '60s Mississippi Movement

Diane Nash *(1938–)*
American SNCC and SCLC activist and official, strategist, organizer

Edgar Nixon *(1899–1987)*
Montgomery Bus Boycott organizer, civil rights activist

James Orange *(1942–2008)*
American SCLC activist and organizer, a voting rights movement leader, trade unionist

Emmeline Pankhurst *(1858-1928)*
founder and leader of the British Suffragette Movement

Rosa Parks *(1913–2005)*
American NAACP official, activist, Montgomery Bus Boycott inspiration

Alice Paul *(1885–1977)*
American 1910s Women's Voting Rights Movement leader, strategist, and organizer

Thomas Paine *(1737-1809)*
English-American activist, author, theorist, wrote Rights of Man

Elizabeth Peratrovich *(1911–1958)*
Alaska activist for native people

A. Philip Randolph *(1889–1979)*
American labor and civil rights movement leader

Amelia Boynton Robinson *(1911–)*
Selma Voting Rights Movement activist and early leader

Jo Ann Robinson *(1912–1992)*
Montgomery Bus Boycott activist.

Eleanor Roosevelt *(1884–1962)*
women's rights and human rights activist both in the United States and in the United Nations

Bayard Rustin *(1912–1987)*
American civil rights activist

Aung San Suu Kyi *(1945–)*
Burmese Politician, former political prisoner, democracy and human rights activist

Sonia Schlesin *(1888–1956)*
worked with Mohandas Gandhi in South Africa and led his movements there when he was absent.

Al Sharpton *(1954–)*
American clergyman, activist, media

Charles Sherrod *(1937–)*
American civil rights activist, SNCC leader

Judy Shepard *(1952–)*
gay rights activist, public speaker

Kate Sheppard *(1847–1934)*
New Zealand suffragist in first country to have universal suffrage

Fred Shuttlesworth *(1922–2011)*
American clergyman, activist, SCLC co-founder, initiated the Birmingham Movement

Lysander Spooner *(1808–1887)*
American abolitionist, writer, anarchist, proponent of Jury nullification

Elizabeth Cady Stanton *(1815–1902)*
American women's suffrage/women's rights leader

Gloria Steinem *(1934–)*
American writer, activist, feminist

Lucy Stone *(1818–1893)*
American women's suffrage/voting rights leader

Thich Quang Duc *(1897–1963)*
Vietnamese monk, freedom of religion self-martyr

Desmond Tutu *(1931–)*
South African anti-apartheid organizer, advocate, inspiration

Karl Heinrich Ulrichs *(1825-1895)*
German writer, organizer, and the pioneer of the modern LGBT rights movement.

C.T. Vivian *(1924–)*
American student civil rights leader, SNCC and SCLC activist

Wyatt Tee Walker *(1929–)*
American activist and organizer with NAACP, CORE, and SCLC

Booker T. Washington *(1865-1915)*

Ida B. Wells *(1862–1931)*
American journalist, early activist in 20th Century Civil Rights Movement, women's suffrage/voting rights activist

Walter Francis White *(1895–1955)*
American NAACP executive secretary

Elie Wiesel *(1928–)*
Jewish rights leader

William Wilberforce *(1759-1833)*
leader of English abolition movement

Roy Wilkins *(1901–1981)*
American NAACP executive secretary/executive director

Frances Willard *(1839–1898)*
American women's rights activist, suffrage leader

Hosea Williams *(1926–2000)*
American civil rights activist, an SCLC organizer and strategist

Victoria Woodhull *(1838–1927)*
American suffragette organizer, women's rights leader

Malcolm X *(1925–1965)*
American author, speaker, activist, inspiration

Andrew Young *(1932–)*
American SCLC activist and executive director

Whitney M. Young, Jr. *(1921–1971)*
Exec. Director National Urban League, advisor to U.S. Presidents

Presidents and Vice-Presidents

1. **George Washington** *(1789-1797)*
   John Adams *(1789-1797)*

2. **John Adams** *(1797-1801)*
   Thomas Jefferson *(1797-1801)*

3. **Thomas Jefferson** *(1801-1809)*
   Aaron Burr *(1801-1805)*
   George Clinton *(1805-1809)*

4. **James Madison** *(1809-1817)*
   George Clinton *(1809-1812)*
   None (1812-1813)
   Elbridge Gerry *(1813-1814)*
   None (1814-1817)

5. **James Monroe** *(1817-1825)*
   Daniel D. Tompkins *(1817-1825)*

6. **John Quincy Adams** *(1825-1829)*
   John C. Calhoun *(1825-1829)*

7. **Andrew Jackson** *(1829-1837)*
   John C. Calhoun *(1829-1832)*
   None (1832-1833)
   Martin Van Buren *(1833-1837)*

8. **Martin Van Buren** *(1837-1841)*
   Richard M. Johnson *(1837-1841)*

9. **William Henry Harrison** *(1841)*
   John Tyler *(1841)*

10. **John Tyler** *(1841-1845)*
    None (1841-1845)

11. **James K. Polk** *(1845-1849)*
    George M. Dallas *(1845-1849)*

12. **Zachary Taylor** *(1849-1850)*
    Millard Fillmore *(1849-1850)*

13. **Millard Fillmore** *(1850-1853)*
    None *(1850-1853)*

14. **Franklin Pierce** *(1853-1857)*
    William King *(1853)*
    None (1853-1857)

15. **James Buchanan** *(1857-1861)*
    John C. Breckinridge *(1857-1861)*

16. **Abraham Lincoln** *(1861-1865)*
    Hannibal Hamlin *(1861-1865)*
    Andrew Johnson *(1865)*

17. **Andrew Johnson** *(1865-1869)*
    None *(1865-1869)*

18. **Ulysses S. Grant** *(1869-1877)*
    Schuyler Colfax *(1869-1873)*
    Henry Wilson *(1873-1875)*
    None (1875-1877)

19. **Rutherford B. Hayes** *(1877-1881)*
    William Wheeler *(1877-1881)*

20. **James A. Garfield** *(1881)*
Chester Arthur *(1881)*

21. **Chester Arthur** *(1881-1885)*
None (1881-1885)

22. **Grover Cleveland** *(1885-1889)*
Thomas Hendricks *(1885)*
None (1885-1889)

23. **Benjamin Harrison** *(1889-1893)*
Levi P. Morton *(1889-1893)*

24. **Grover Cleveland** *(1893-1897)*
Adlai E. Stevenson *(1893-1897)*

25. **William McKinley** *(1897-1901)*
Garret Hobart *(1897-1899)*
None (1899-1901)
Theodore Roosevelt *(1901)*

26. **Theodore Roosevelt** *(1901-1909)*
None (1901-1905)
Charles Fairbanks *(1905-1909)*

27. **William Howard Taft** *(1909-1913)*
James S. Sherman *(1909-1912)*
None (1912-1913)

28. **Woodrow Wilson** *(1913-1921)*
Thomas R. Marshall *(1913-1921)*

29. **Warren G. Harding** *(1921-1923)*
Calvin Coolidge *(1921-1923)*

30. **Calvin Coolidge** *(1923-1929)*
    None (1923-1925)
    Charles Dawes *(1925-1929)*

31. **Herbert Hoover** *(1929-1933)*
    Charles Curtis *(1929-1933)*

32. **Franklin D. Roosevelt** *(1933-1945)*
    John Nance Garner *(1933-1941)*
    Henry A. Wallace *(1941-1945)*
    Harry S. Truman *(1945)*

33. **Harry S Truman** *(1945-1953)*
    None (1945-1949)
    Alben Barkley *(1949-1953)*

34. **Dwight D. Eisenhower** *(1953-1961)*
    Richard Nixon *(1953-1961)*

35. **John F. Kennedy** *(1961-1963)*
    Lyndon B. Johnson *(1961-1963)*

36. **Lyndon B. Johnson** *(1963-1969)*
    None (1963-1965)
    Hubert Humphrey *(1965-1969)*

37. **Richard Nixon** *(1969-1974)*
    Spiro Agnew *(1969-1973)*
    None (1973)
    Gerald Ford *(1973-1974)*

38. **Gerald Ford** *(1974-1977)*
    None (1974)
    Nelson Rockefeller *(1974-1977)*

39. **Jimmy Carter** *(1977-1981)*
     Walter Mondale *(1977-1981)*

40. **Ronald Reagan** *(1981-1989)*
     George Bush *(1981-1989)*

41. **George Bush** *(1989-1993)*
     Dan Quayle *(1989-1993)*

42. **Bill Clinton** *(1993-2001)*
     Al Gore *(1993-2001)*

43. **George W. Bush** *(2001-2009)*
     Dick Cheney *(2001-2009)*

44. **Barack Obama** *(2009-present)*
     Joe Biden *(2009-present)*

Map of The United States

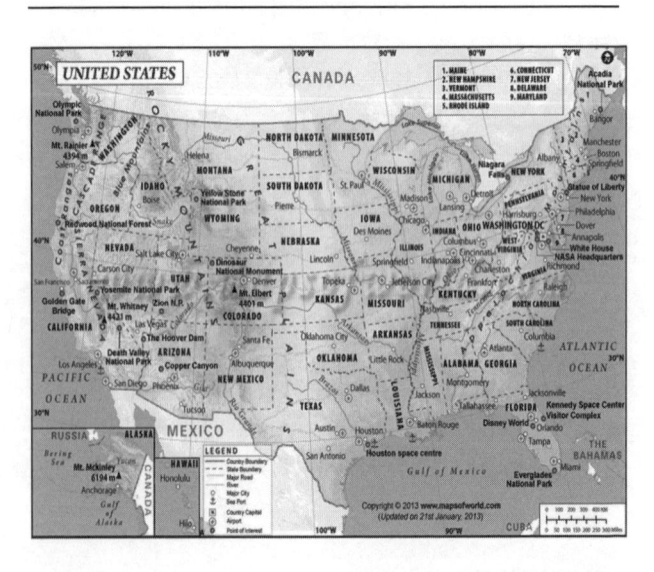

Cardinal Directions

The four **cardinal directions** or **cardinal points** are the directions of north, east, south, and west, commonly denoted by their initials: N, E, S, W. East and west are at right angles to north and south, with east being in the clockwise direction of rotation from north and west being directly opposite east. Intermediate points between the four cardinal directions form the points of the compass. The intermediate (intercardinal, or ordinal) directions are northeast (NE), southeast (SE), southwest (SW), and northwest (NW). Further, the intermediate direction of every set of intercardinal and cardinal direction is called a secondary-intercardinal direction, the eight shortest points in the compass rose to the right, i.e. NNE, ENE, ESE, and so on.

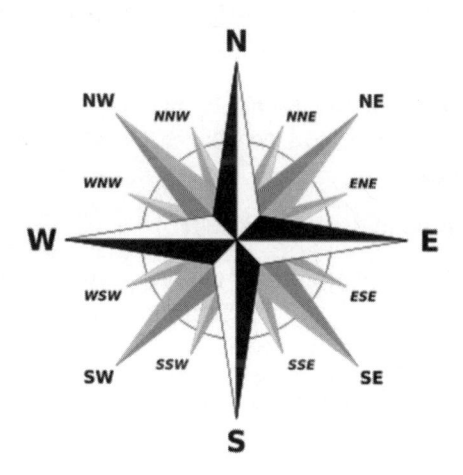

Social Study Glossary Terms

A

Absolute Advantage: exists in the production of a good when one country can produce a good more efficiently than another country.

Absolute Location: the exact position on the globe using addresses, grid coordinates, or the imaginary lines of longitude and latitude.

Acid rain: a type of polluted rain, produced when acids from smokestacks combine with water vapor that can harm lakes, forests, and human health.

Adapt: to change or tailor something to fit, humans change their environment or their way of doing something to fit their current needs or goals.

Advertising: information provided to encourage the purchase or use of a good, service or idea by emphasizing its positive qualities.

Affirmative Action: efforts to recruit or hire members of underrepresented groups, such as women and minorities.

Allegiance: devotion or loyalty.

Allocation: the process of choosing which needs will be satisfied and how much of our resources we will use to satisfy them.

Alternative Courses of Action: the other choice that could have been made which are inherent in every decision.

Altitude: the height of a thing above sea level or above the earth's surface.

Amendment (to the U.S. Constitution): changes in, or additions to, a constitution. Proposed by a two-thirds vote of both houses of Congress or at the request of two-thirds of the state legislatures. Ratified by approval of three-fourths of the states.

American Influence on Foreign Countries: as the most powerful nation and economy in the world the United States affects the cultures, economies, and politics of nations worldwide. When other nations seek access to and become part of the lucrative U.S. market their own economies, cultures and politics are affected by American culture and values.

American Political System/Presidential System: a system of government in which the legislative and executive branches operate independently of each other and in which power is distributed through a system of checks and balances.

Amnesty: a general pardon granted by a government, especially for political offenses.

Analog: a face clock with hands.

Anarchy: Absence of any form of political authority. A state of lawlessness, confusion, and disorder (usually resulting from a failure of government.)

Ancient history: history of people living from the beginnings of human society through 300 CE

Apartheid: policy of separation of the races enforced by law

Appellate court: a court authorized to hear appeals

Apportionment: the distribution of legislative seats according to population

Arbitration: Settlement of a dispute by the decision of a judge, umpire or committee.

Articles of Confederation: The first document created to govern the newly formed government after the American Revolution. It created a "firm league of friendship" among the 13 original states. The states agreed to send delegates to a Confederation Congress. Each state had one vote in Congress.

Artifact: Things made by humans, and used by archaeologists and historians to recreate a picture of the past.

Authority: Right to control or direct the actions of others, legitimized by law, morality, custom, or consent.

B

Bar Graph: A means of displaying data using the length of "bars" to represent the values of the data being displayed.

Barter: The direct trading of goods and services between people without the use of money.

Beliefs: Opinions about what is considered to be true and trustworthy.

Benefits: Something of value, a benefit can be tangible like a gift or money, or intangible like satisfaction.

Bias: An unfair act or policy resulting from prejudice.

Bigotry: Intolerance and prejudice; obstinate and unreasoning attachment to one's own belief and opinions, with narrow-minded intolerance of beliefs opposed to them

Biography: A narrative account of a person's life.

Bill of Rights: First ten amendments to the Constitution ratified in 1791, these amendments limit governmental power and protect basic rights and liberties of individuals.

Biome: A major regional or global biotic community, such as a grassland or desert, characterized chiefly by the dominant forms of plant life and prevailing climate.

Bipartisan: Supported by members of two parties, especially two major political parties

Boundary: The limit or extent within which a system exists or functions, including a social group, at state, or physical feature.

Branches of Government: Established in the U.S. Constitution to divide the power of government between legislative, executive and judicial branches

Brown v. Board of Education of Topeka (1954): Supreme Court case that declared that "separate-but-equal" educational facilities are inherently unequal and therefore a violation of equal protection of the law guaranteed by the Fourteenth Amendment.

C

Calendar: A table showing the days, weeks, and months of at least one specific year.

Campaign: The overall effort a candidate makes to win votes through speeches, press conferences, and advertising.

Campaigns: Activities planned to achieve a certain goal as in electing a candidate or establishing a public policy.

Campaign finance reforms: How money is collected and spent in campaigns for public office is subject to rules. Many groups believe that a major change in those rules is necessary to limit the amount of money that any person or group can donate to a political campaign with the goal being to limit the influence any person or group will have after the election to influence the office holder they helped to elect.

Capital: Cash, goods, natural resources, or human skills that are used to produce income.

Capital Equipment: Manufactured equipment used in the production of goods and services.

Capital Resources: Goods made by people and used to produce other goods and services (also called intermediate goods).

Capitalism: Economic system characterized by the following: private property ownership exists; individuals and companies are allowed to compete for their own economic gain; and free market forces determine the prices of goods and services.

Cartel: Explicit forms of collusion concerned with product price, output, service, or sales.

Cash: Currency and coins

Caucus: A meeting, especially a preliminary meeting, of persons belonging to a party, to nominate candidates for public office, or to select delegates to a nominating convention, or to confer regarding measures of party policy; a political primary meeting.

Census: An official, usually periodic enumeration of a population, often including the collection of related demographic information. As required by the Constitution, the census of the population of the United States takes place every 10 years.

Century: One hundred years.

Certificates of Deposit (CD): These offer a guaranteed rate of interest for a specified term, usually one year. The institution generally requires that you keep your money in the account until the term ends. The institution may pay a higher rate of interest than for a savings or other account. Typically, the longer the term, the higher the interest

Characteristics: A special quality or feature; whatever distinguishes one person or thing from others.

Checking Accounts: Deposits in a checking account give individuals quick, convenient, and immediate access to money in their account. Money is accessed through the writing of a check, which transfers money to the person or business named. Some checking accounts pay interest (NOW accounts), but most do not institutions may impose fees on checking accounts, along with a charge for the checks.

Checks and Balances: Constitutional mechanisms that authorize each branch of government to share powers with the other branches and thereby check their activities. For example, the president may veto legislation passed by Congress, the Senate must confirm major executive appointments, and the courts may declare acts of Congress unconstitutional.

Chlorofluorocarbons: A series of hydrocarbons containing both chlorine and fluorine. These have been used as refrigerants, blowing agents, cleaning fluids, solvents, and as fire extinguishing agents. They have been shown to cause stratospheric ozone depletion and have been banned for many uses.

Choropleth map: Maps that display data by using colors or shading to represent distinct categories of qualities or quantities.

Choice: What someone must make when faced with two or more alternative uses for a resource, also called an economic choice.

Chronological order: Arranged in order of time occurrence.

Circle Graph: Used to display data that adds up to 100%

Circular Flow: The flow of money from businesses to households and government, from households to businesses and government, and from government to households and business.

Citizen's responsibilities and conduct: Actions expected of citizens in their daily conduct such as upholding the values and principles of the Constitution, obeying the law, voting and participating in the civic life of the community.

Citizenship: Status of being a member of a nation, one who owes allegiance to the government and is entitled to its protection and to political rights.

City Council: The equivalent of the legislative branch for a city. City-state - A self-governing city, often with surrounding lands it governs.

Civil court: The place where disputes between people, or between people and the government are resolved.

Civilization: The type of culture and society developed by a particular nation or region or in a particular epoch: The ways in which people organize themselves.

Civil Rights: Protections and privileges given to all U.S. citizens by the Constitution and Bill of rights

Climate: The temperature, precipitation, winds, etc. that characterize a region. Long- term trends in weather elements and atmospheric conditions.

Coin: Money issued by a government in the form of a metal disk.

Colony: A group of emigrants or their descendants who settle in a distant territory but remain subject to or closely associated with the parent country.

Command Economies: An economy in which the government makes the decisions about what, where, how and how much is produced and finally who will get what is produced.

Common Good: Involves individual citizens having the commitment and motivation (that they accept as their obligation) to promote the welfare of the community (even if they must sacrifice their own time, personal preferences or money) to work together with other members for the greater benefit of all.

Communism: The final state of social evolution according to Marx, in which the state has withered away and economic goods are distributed according to need.

Communication: The exchange of thoughts messages and or information.

Community: A group of people living in the same locality and under the same government.

Community Characteristic: A feature that helps to define, describe, or distinguish one community from another.

Comparative advantage: The principle that states that a country benefits from specializing in the production of goods at which it is relatively most efficient.

Comparison: An examination of two or more objects, ideas, locations, concepts, or individuals to discover the similarities and differences.

Compass rose: Orientation graphic that indicates the direction north on a map or globe.

Competitive Markets: Markets with many buyers and sellers where not one person or firm controls prices or the number of products for sale.

Complementary Goods: Goods that are jointly consumed. The consumption of one enhances the consumption of the other (examples hot dogs/hotdog buns; left shoe/right shoe; snow skis and snow clothing).

Composite region: A region that shares more than one characteristic or function e.g., Midwest-agricultural region, Midwest-industrial region, urban-industrial regions

Compromise of 1850: Had four parts–first, California was allowed to enter the Union as a free state; second, the rest of the Mexican Cession was divided into the territories of New Mexico and Utah (in each territory, voters would decide the slavery question according to popular sovereignty); third, the slave trade was ended in Washington, D.C., the nation's capitol (Congress, however, declared that it had no power to ban the slave trade between slave states; fourth, a strict new fugitive slave law was passed.

Conflict: An open clash between two opposing groups, individuals, or nations regarding an ideology or a course of action.

Conflict and cooperation: A recurring theme of social studies that represents the opportunities for people in communities, nations, regions or worldwide to engage in activities in which they openly clash with one another while retaining the capacity at other times to work together towards accomplishing common goals.

Conflicting viewpoint: A position taken by one individual group, or nation, which is in opposition to the position of another individual, group or nation.

Consensus: A point reached in a negotiation where a general agreement of all or most of the people consulted is achieved

Constitution: The system of fundamental laws and principles that prescribes the nature, functions, and limits of a government or another institution. The fundamental law of the United States, framed in 1787, ratified in 1789, and variously amended since then.

Constitutional guarantee: The promises or assurances given to the people of the nation in their written constitution, which cannot be taken away without the due process of law.

Consumer: A customer who buys the products or services a business produces.

Consumer Credit: Ability to buy goods or services now and pay later by installment payments.

Consumer Goods: Items that are made for final consumption (i.e., not used by business to produce other goods or services)

Consumer Spending: Purchase of consumer goods and services.

Contemporary factors: Something that belongs to the same time period as the event, which contributes causally to the event, like the present efficiency and abundance in the production of wheat in the United States allows us to sell wheat to other countries who need it.

Continent: One of seven large landmasses on the Earth, which separates the oceans

Core Democratic Values: Fundamental beliefs and constitutional principles outlined in the Declaration of independence and/or the United States Constitution and other important writings of the nation such as Supreme Court decisions.

Corporation: An organization of people legally bound together by a charter to conduct some type of business.

Costs: The total money, time and resources associated with a purchase or activity.

Costs of Production: All resources used in producing goods and services, for which their owners receive payment.

Country: A sovereign nation.

County: The largest territorial division of a state.

Coup d' etat: The sudden overthrow of a government by usually a small group of persons in or previously in positions of authority

Crimes against humanity: Actions that are agreed to be so universally abhorrent that they are determined to be unacceptable by all people regardless of culture and for which people seek to have the perpetrators punished on behalf of humanity.

Criminal court: The place where cases are heard for those accused of breaking a law

Criminal procedure: A set of established steps taken when the government is preparing a criminal prosecution to bring a person accused of breaking a law to trial, which includes due process for the accused.

Crusade: Any of the military expeditions undertaken by European Christians in the 11th, 12th, and 13th centuries to recover the Holy Land from the Muslims. Also, a vigorous concerted movement for a cause or against an abuse.

Culture: The values, beliefs and perceptions of the world that are learned and are shared by members of a community or society, and which they use to interpret experience and to generate behavior, and that are reflected in their own behavior.

Cultural diffusion: The spread of linguistic or cultural practices or innovations (including ideas and beliefs) within a culture or from one culture to another.

Cultural geography: The study of how people use space and interact with their environment.

Cultural stability and change: An important theme in social studies, particularly in geography and history, which addresses how different societies maintain the stability of their culture and how they deal with the inevitable difficulties associated with change as a result of interactions with other cultures or changes in prevailing values.

Cultural Relativism: The idea that each culture's features should be understood in terms of that culture's history, environment, values, and views of its people, and that it is ethnocentric or biased, as well as uninformed, to judge another culture by the standards of one's own culture.

Culture: Learned behavior of people, which includes their belief systems and languages, their social relationships, their institutions and organizations, and their material goods (food, clothing, buildings, tools, and machines).

Currency: Paper money with a specified value, issued by the government or a central bank.

Currency Exchange: The comparative value of foreign currencies.

D

Decade: Ten years.

Deciduous: Type of tree that loses its leaves during portions of the year, usually beginning in the autumn months

Decision: A conclusion or judgment reached after consideration of alternatives.

Decision Matrix: A table comparing possible decisions.

Declaration of Independence: The declaration of the Congress of the Thirteen United States of America, on the 4th of July, 1776, by which they formally declared that these colonies were free and independent States, not subject to the government of Great Britain.

Defining Characteristic: Shared patterns of life, which characterize a period of history.

Deflation: A decline in general price levels, often caused by a reduction in the supply of money or credit.

Deforestation: The clearing or destruction of forests, generally for the purposes of timber extraction, agricultural expansion, cattle raising and in drier climates an increase demand for firewood.

Delegated Powers: Powers granted to the national government under the Constitution, as enumerated in Articles, II, III, and I

Demagogue: A leader who obtains power by means of impassioned appeals to the emotions and prejudices of the populace.

Demand: The desire and ability of individuals to purchase economic goods or services at the market price; along with supply, one of the two key determinants of price.

Democracy: A system of government in which political authority is held by the people; typically feature constitutional governments where the majority rules, a belief in individual liberty and in equal rights for all people, freedom of expression, political freedom, and freedom of choice.

Demography: The study that emphasizes statistics to look at human population distribution, population density, and trends in population

Describe: To tell the who, what, when or where about something

Desegregation: To abolish or eliminate segregation; to open (a school or workplace, for example) to members of all races or ethnic groups, especially by force of law; to become open to members of all races or ethnic groups.

Desert: An area with little precipitation or where evaporation exceeds precipitation and thus includes sparse vegetation

Desertification: A process by which desert-like conditions are created by a loss of plant cover and soil due to human activity and climatic changes in arid and semi-arid regions

Dictator: A ruler with absolute power.

Digital clock: clock, which only uses numbers to tell the time.

Discrimination: Treatment based on class or category rather than individual merit.

Disenfranchised: Deprived of the rights of citizenship especially the right to vote

Disparities: Lack of equality.

Dispute: A disagreement or argument about something important

Distributor: A firm that sells and delivers merchandise to retail stores or acts as an intermediary in business.

Distribution: The delivery of merchandise to retail stores.

Diversity: Variety in culture and ethnic background, race and belief is not only permissible but also desirable and beneficial in a pluralistic society.

Doctrine: A principle or body of principles presented for acceptance or belief, as by a religious, political, scientific, or philosophic group; dogma, e.g., Monroe Doctrine

Domestic: Of one's own country; not foreign.

Domestic Economy: Activities dealing with the production and distribution of goods and services within ones own country.

Dred Scott v. Sanford: Dred Scott Decision of 1857: The Supreme Court ruled that Dred Scott could not file a lawsuit because, as a black, he was not a citizen. The justices also agreed that slaves were property. They also ruled that Congress did not have the power to outlaw slavery in any territory.

Due Process of Law: Right of every citizen to be protected against arbitrary action by government; the government must use fair procedures to gather information and make decisions in order to protect the rights of individuals and the interests of society.

E

Earning: Activities people engage in to acquire resources. Also, income after taxes is deducted.

Early Inhabitants: People who first lived in a place.

Economic and political connections: The relationship between the government of a state, nation or municipality and its economic system, such as regulation of banking, local ordinances, or worker safety.

Economic Development: Actions taken to improve the ability of people to more productively use capital, natural and human resources in the production of goods and services.

Economic Dispute: A disagreement over how resources will be used.

Economic Freedom: The right to acquire, use, transfer and dispose of private property without unreasonable governmental interference; the right to seek employment wherever one pleases; to change employment at will; and to engage in any lawful economic activity.

Economic geography: The study of how people use space and interact with their environment to answer the basic economic questions of production and distribution.

Economic Goals of Government: In the mixed economy of the United States government has six broad goals: economic growth, more and better goods and services produced; full employment, everyone who wants to work should have a job; price stability, stable prices that do not rise dramatically, economic freedom, individuals should be free to make their own economic decisions; fair distribution of wealth, an agreement in principle that it is undesirable for any group to suffer extreme poverty while others enjoy extreme wealth; and economic security, government aid for those who are sick, disabled, or aged.

Economic Growth: The change in the level of economic activity from one year to another.

Economic Incentives: Factors that motivate the behavior of households and business, prices, profits, and losses act as incentives for participants to take action in a market economy.

Economic Indicators: The leading indicators include the money supply, stock prices, consumer expectations, commodity (raw materials, farm products) prices, the average work week, new unemployment claims, new building permits, new orders for consumer goods, new orders for capital goods, unfilled orders, and back-logged deliveries.

Economic Institutions, household, government, business, banks, labor unions: An organization founded and united for a specific economic purpose, i.e.; making decisions about the consumption and production of resources.

Economic Measurement: Tracking the change in the level of economic activity from one time period to another. Standard economic measurements are the GDP, housing starts, unemployment rates, and the Consumer Price Index.

Economic Roles of Government: In the mixed economy of the United States government has six broad goals: economic growth, more and better goods and services produced; full employment, everyone who wants to work should have a job; price stability, stable prices that do not rise dramatically, economic freedom, individuals should be free to make their own economic decisions; fair distribution of wealth, an agreement in principle that it is undesirable for any group to suffer extreme poverty while others enjoy extreme wealth; and economic security, government aid for those who are sick, disabled, or aged.

Economic System: The way a society organizes the production, consumption, and distribution of goods and services.

Economic Trends: The current general direction of movement of an economic indicator. Trends can track consumer purchases and production, supply and demand, GDP, prices, and interest rates

Economics:

1. Having to do with the production, distribution, and consumption of goods and services.
2. The management of the income, supplies, and expenses of household, government, etc.

Ecosystems (ecological system): A system formed by the interaction of all living organisms (plants, animals, and humans) with each other and with the physical and chemical factors of the environment in which they live.

Electoral college: The group of people selected by each state that elect the president and Vice President of the United States. The number of votes each states receives is determined by the number of representatives they have in Congress (the number of their state's Representatives plus their two Senators).

Elevation: The height on the earth's surface above or below sea level

Emigrant: Emigrant and emigration have reference to the country from which the migration is made; the correlative words immigrant and immigration have reference to the country into which the migration is made, the former marking the going out from a country, the latter the coming into it.

Emotion: Arousal that is interpreted in relation to a situation and results in expressive behavior.

Endowed: Provided with/for; in the Declaration of Independence: "...that they are endowed by their creator with certain unalienable rights..." i.e. rights are provided to each person by their creator and can neither be given or taken away by a person or the government

English Bill of Rights: A law passed by Parliament in 1689 that forms the foundation of Britain's unwritten constitution. The bill prohibited the monarchy from suspending laws, levying taxes or maintaining an army in peacetime without consent of Parliament.

Enslaved people: Individuals whose liberty has been taken away and are forced to work for others without compensation as property

Entrepreneur: Individual who takes the risk of producing a product for a profit Environment – the natural or human surrounding in which living things interact.

EPA: Environmental Protection Agency

Equality: Everyone should get the same treatment regardless of where their parents or grandparents were born, their race or religion, or how much money they have, citizens all have political, social, and economic equality.

Era: A period of time in history.

Ethical consideration: A set of moral standards that is a factor when making decisions or judgments.

Ethics: Standards of right and wrong; morals.

Ethnic Group: People who share a common cultural background, including ancestry and language.

Ethnic Cleansing: The removal or extermination of a racial or cultural group.

Ethnography: The systematic description of a particular culture based on first-hand observation. (The person who does ethnography is called an ethnographer).

Ethnocentrism: Looking at the world from the perspective of one's own culture; the attitude or belief that the ways of one's own culture are the best or only proper ones. Other ways are therefore judged wrong or immoral, not simply different.

Ethnicity: One's cultural identity (NOT biological identity).

Evaluate: Make judgments about the value of ideas or materials.

Exchange: Giving one thing in return for some other thing.

Excise tax: A Federal or state tax imposed on the manufacture and distribution of certain non-essential consumer goods.

Executive Branch: Carries out and enforces laws to protect individual rights and promote the common good.

Executive Power: Power of the president governor or mayor to implement and enforce laws.

Explain: To give reasons for why something happens

Exports: Goods or services produced in one nation but sold to buyers in another nation.

F

Factors of Production: Resources used by businesses to produce goods and services; natural resources, human capital, capital and entrepreneurship

Federal: Anything pertaining to the national government, but not the state or local government.

Federal Courts: Article III of the Constitution gives the federal courts jurisdiction— the authority to hear and decide a case—only in certain specific areas. These are cases that involve one of the following: The Constitution, federal laws, admiralty and maritime laws, disputes in which the United States government is involved, controversies between sates, controversies between citizens of different states, Disputes involving foreign governments and United States ambassadors, ministers, and consuls serving in foreign countries.

Federal Judiciary: Nine members of the U.S. Supreme Court and approximately five hundred judges appointed by the president and approved by the Senate for the federal courts

Federal Reserve System (the Fed): The central banking system in the United States. It regulates money and banking in the United States.

Federalism: Power is shared between two sets of governmental institutions, those of the states and those of the central or federal authorities, as stipulated by the Constitution

Fees: Charges for services rendered.

Feudal system: Introduced to England by William I -The Conqueror. In a feudal system the King owned all the land. The King as his personal property kept one quarter, some was given to the church and the rest was rented out. In this system a lord swears allegiance to the king in return for protection. A lord took in serfs who paid homage to him and took the same oath. This system would continue to the lower and lower classes that would work for fiefs or land. The Feudal System lasted in England until the Tudor period.

Filibuster: The use of obstructionist tactics, especially prolonged speechmaking, for the purpose of delaying legislative action.

Fiscal Policy: Decisions by the President and Congress, usually relating to taxation and government spending, with the goals of full employment, price stability, and economic growth

Five Themes of Geography:
- **Location:** Includes both absolute and relative. Absolute location: expressed in terms of the latitude and longitude identifies a place's exact location on the earth. Relative location: describes where a place is in relation to other places.

- **Place:** Particular city, village, or area with distinctive physical and human characteristics that distinguishes it from other places.

- **Human Environment/Interaction:** How people change their surroundings like clearing land to make farms; and how people adapt to their environment like building homes with insulation and central heating in cold climates.

- **Movement:** The moving of people, ideas, information, and products around the world.

- **Region:** An area with one or more common characteristics or features, which gives it a measure of homogeneity and makes it different from surrounding areas.

Fluorocarbons: Any of various chemically inert compounds containing carbon and fluoride used chiefly as lubricants and refrigerants and in making resins plastics. (see chlorofluorocarbons)

Foreign market: When buyers and sellers from different countries make transactions, directly or via intermediaries.

Foreign policy: When dealing with other nations, the systematic collection of practices, regulations, and rules of procedure and conduct followed by the Federal Government.

Forensic Anthropology: A special field within Physical Anthropology that uses knowledge of the human skeleton to help crimes and other legal issues. Forensic anthropologists, for example, have been working to identify the skeletal traces recovered from the 9-11 disasters.

Forms of Taxation: Forms of taxation: taxes are charges imposed by the government on people or property for public purposes. Taxes take different forms like the benefit principle (gasoline taxes for road construction), progressive taxes, regressive taxes, proportional taxes, direct taxes, indirect taxes, income taxes, sales taxes, excise taxes (levied on a specific item), property taxes estate and gift taxes, tariffs and social security tax.

Free Market Economy: An economy in which individuals decide the economic questions in the market place.

Freedom: Being able to act without interference or control by another; right to believe in what you want, right to choose own friends, and have own ideas and opinions, to express own ideas in public, the right for people to meet in groups, the right to have any lawful job or business.

Fundamentalism: Fundamentalism can be broadly defined as a strict and literal adherence to a set of basic principles and specific beliefs. Although many, if not most forms of fundamentalism are religious, by no means are all religious people fundamentalists. The adherence to certain beliefs seen in fundamentalism is so strong, that the presentation of evidence that contradicts these beliefs leads to no reassessment of them, on the part of the fundamentalist.

G

Genocide: The extermination of a cultural or racial group.

Geography: An integrated discipline that brings together the physical and human dimensions of the world in the study of people, place, and environment focusing on the earth's surface and the processes that shape it, the relationships between people and environments, and the connections between people and places.

Gideon v. Wainwright (1963): The Supreme Court ruled that in federal and state criminal cases involving serious criminal cases involving serious crimes, the court must appoint a lawyer to represent an accused person who cannot afford one. In 1972 the Supreme Court extended the right to counsel even further. It ruled that an accused person cannot be sent to jail for any offense unless he or she has either been represented by counsel or voluntarily given up that right. This ruling covers all cases that could involve imprisonment, no matter how minor the crime.

GIS global information systems: A geographic database that contains information about the distribution of physical and human characteristics of places or areas.

Good character: The moral quality of one's decisions and behavior that is generally accepted as positive

Goods: Objects that can be held or touched that can satisfy people's wants.

Globalization: Refers to the many ways in which people are being drawn together not only by their own movements but also through the flow of goods/services, capital, and ideas/information. Globalization also includes the impact that increased human interactions have on the natural environment.

Global warming: The theory that Earth's atmosphere is gradually warming due to the buildup of carbon dioxide in the lower atmosphere caused by human activity such as the burning of coal

Governor: The chief executive of a state government who is elected by the state's voters.

Government: An institution that determines and enforces a society's laws. The size and nature of a government varies according to the society it governs.

Government Regulation: A rule, law, statute or ordinance, through which the government monitors the use of wealth or property by individuals, groups or businesses.

Graphic Data: Information organized in a pictorial way like a chart, graph or map.

Grasslands: Middle-latitude grasslands are located between the temperate forests and desert biomes. Because of a semiarid climate, grasslands usually do not have tree cover except along rivers. Wetter grasslands supporting taller grasses are prairies and drier desert margin grassland regions are called steppes

Greenhouse Effect: The warming of the earth caused by the buildup of carbon dioxide in the lower atmosphere, possibly as the result of human industrial activity

Gross Domestic Product (GDP): The total dollar value of all final goods and services produced in a country in a given year equals the total consumer, investment and government spending, plus the value of exports minus the value of imports.

Gross National Product (GNP): Calculated by adjusting the GDP to include income accruing to domestic residents as a result of investments abroad minus the income earned in domestic markets accruing to foreigners abroad.

H

Habitat: A place where a plant or animal naturally or normally lives and grows.

Hills: Landform features that may have steep slopes but lower in elevation and characterized by less local relief than a mountain

Households: Individual or family units.

Human Capital: The people who perform the work in the production of goods and services and the skills, which they have.

Human Characteristics of Place: Things that humans do to change the environment or natural surroundings (e.g., bridges, roads, and buildings). Also the language, culture, food and religions of a place.

Human Environment/Interaction: How people adapt their lives to some environmental conditions; how people protect themselves from cold climates; how people will change their natural environment.

Human Resources: Quantity and quality of human effort directed toward producing goods and services (also called labor or human capital).

Human rights: The basic rights and freedoms to which all humans are entitled, often held to include the right to life and liberty, freedom of thought and expression, and equality before the law.

Hydrologic Cycle: The continuous circulation of water from the oceans, ice sheets, lithosphere, atmosphere, and all living things in the biosphere.

I

Identify: To recognize and name an object, person, or idea.

Ideas: Something, such as a thought or concept, that potentially or actually exists in the mind as a product of mental activity, an opinion, conviction, or principle.

Identify: To name something

Immigration: To enter and settle in a country or region to which one is not native.

Imports: Goods and services that consumers in one country buy from producers in another country.

Inalienable: (also unalienable) Rights that cannot be given or taken away.

Incentives: Factors that motivate and influence the behavior of households and businesses; prices, profits, and losses act as incentives for participants to take action in a market economy.

Indentured servitude: A contract between two people where one party agrees to work without any or minimal compensation to pay back money or an opportunity provided by the other

Indigenous: Originating and living or occurring naturally in an area or environment e.g., indigenous plants or the indigenous people of a country

Income Taxes: Taxes paid by households and business firms on the income they receive.

Indian Removal Act (1830): Native Americans were forced to sign treaties agreeing to move west of the Mississippi.

Individual choice: Decisions made by people acting separately.

Individual Ownership: A business owned and managed by one individual who assumes all risk of loss and gets all the profit.

Individual Rights: Fundamental to American constitutional democracy is the belief that individuals have certain basic rights that are not created by government but which government should protect. These are the right to life, liberty, economic freedom, and the pursuit of happiness. It is the purpose of government to protect these rights, and it may not place unfair or unreasonable restraints on their exercise. Many of these rights are enumerated in the Bill of Rights.

Inflation: An increase in the general level of prices people pay for goods and services. A popular measure of inflation is the consumer price index.

Infringement: Contrary to or violate; go beyond the proper or usual limits.

Innovation: A newly introduced idea, invention or way of doing things that changes the world.

Institutions: Customs, practices, relationships, or behavioral patterns of importance in the life of a community or society: the institutions of marriage and the family. Established organizations or foundations that reflect the culture and beliefs of a people.

Integration: The bringing of people of different

racial or ethnic groups into unrestricted and equal association

Interdependence: People relying on each other in different places or in the same place for ideas, goods, and services.

International: Between or among nations; having to do with the relations between nations.

International Monetary Fund (IMF): An organization set up to lower trade barriers between countries and to stabilize currencies, often by lending money to developing nations.

International Trade: The exchange of goods and services between or among nations.

Interpretation: An explanation of something that is not immediately obvious.

Investment: Purchase of tangible assets, such as machines, factories, or inventories that are used to produce goods and services for the purpose of making a profit.

Investments in Capital Resources: Business purchases of new plant and equipment.

Investment in Human Resources: Activities that increase the skills and knowledge of workers.

Invisible hand: Term used by Adam Smith to describe the natural force that guides free market capitalism through competition for scarce resources.

Islam: A monotheistic religion characterized by the acceptance of the doctrine of submission to God and to Muhammad as the chief and last prophet of God.

J

Jihad: A Muslim holy war or spiritual struggle against infidels (those who do not believe in the doctrines of the Islamic faith)

Jim Crow Laws: The systematic practice of discriminating against and segregating Black people, especially as practiced in the American South from the end of Reconstruction to the mid – 20th century.

Judicial Branch: The Branch of the Federal government responsible for interpreting laws. The Supreme Court heads it. A major responsibility is to protect individual rights and settle conflicts or disputes.

Justice: People should be treated fairly in the distribution of the benefits and burdens of society, the correction of wrongs and injuries, and in the gathering of information and making of decisions.

K

Key: An explanation of the features, colors, or shading on a map or chart

Kinship: The patterns and rules of relationship among people who are linked or related to each other through shared descent from common ancestors or through marriage.

L

Labor: The physical and mental exertion that human beings put into production activities.

Labor force: Those who are working or actively seeking work.

Landform: The shape, form, or nature of a specific physical feature of the earth's surface; e.g., plain, hill, valley, plateau, bay island

Land use: The range of uses of Earth's surface made by humans. Uses are classified as urban, rural, agricultural, forested, etc.

Latitude: A measure of distance north or south of the equator.

Law: A set of rules, issued and enforced by a government that binds every member of society.

Law of Demand: If supply is held constant, an increase in demand leads to an increased market price, while a decrease in demand leads to a decreased market price.

Law of diminishing returns: A point beyond which the application of additional resources yields less than proportional increases in output.

Law of diminishing marginal utility: The principle that as additional units of a product are consumed during a given time period, the additional satisfaction for the consumer decreases

Law of Supply: If demand is held constant, an increase in supply leads to a decreased price, while a decrease in supply leads to increased price.

Learning: A relatively permanent change in behavior that occurs through experience.

Legal: According to the law; permitted by law; lawful

Legend: An explanatory description to the features on a map or chart

Legislative Branch: Passes laws to protect individual rights and promote the common good.

Libertarian party: Libertarians believe in complete liberty, free enterprise, and personal responsibility without the constraints of government. www.lpty.org

Liberty: Includes the freedom to believe what you want, freedom to choose your own friends, and to have your own ideas and opinions, to express your ideas in public, the right for people to meet in groups, and the right to have any lawful job or business.

Life: Each citizen has the right to the protection of their life; individuals right to life should be considered inviolable except in certain highly restricted and extreme circumstances, such as the use of deadly force to protect one's own or others' lives.

Limited Resources: The condition of there not being enough resources to fulfill all wants and needs.

Line graph: A means of displaying data by connecting lines between dots representing the values of a continuous variable.

Lithosphere: The uppermost portion of the solid Earth, including soil, land, and geologic formations

Location: Where something is.

- **Absolute Location:** The exact position on the globe using addresses, grid coordinates, or the imaginary lines of longitude and latitude
- **Relative Location:** The location of a place or region in relation to other places or regions (e.g., northwest of or downstream from).

Longitude: The position of a point on Earth's surface expressed as its angular distance, east or west, from the prime meridian to 180°

Loss: The investment lost in a business when its expenses exceed its income Lumbering – industry involved in cutting timber and selling it.

M

Major World Processes: Population growth, economic development, urbanization, resource use, international trade, global communication, and environmental impact.

Marbury v. Madison (1803): Case in which the Supreme Court held that it had the power of judicial review over acts of Congress.

Market: The place where buyers and sellers come together to make transactions of goods and services.

Market Economy: An economic system based only on the interaction of market forces, such as supply and demand. A true market economy is free of governmental influence, collusion and other external interference, and buyers and sellers making exchanges determine prices

Mediation: To come in to help settle a dispute; be a go between; act in order to bring about an agreement between persons or sides.

Meeting of the Three Worlds: The era of early North American history when the people of North America, Europe, and Africa interact on the North American continent.

Melting pot: Term was coined in the early 1900s by playwright Israel Zangwill in his play The Melting Pot. The term refers to the Zangwill's theory that immigrants to the United States lose their unique national-ethnic identities upon their arrival in the United States and become "Americans".

Millennium: One thousand years.

Minerals: A naturally occurring, homogeneous inorganic solid substance having a definite chemical composition and characteristic crystalline structure, color, and hardness.

Migration: To move from one place to settle in another.

Miranda Rule: An arresting officer's requirements to inform criminal suspects of their rights before questioning.

Mixed Economy: An economy that combines elements of the traditional, market, and command economic models.

Model: A set of assumptions and hypotheses that is a simplified description of reality. Monarchy – a system of government in which the head of state, usually a royal figure (king, queen) is a hereditary position.

Monetary Policy: The regulation of the money supply and interest rates by a central bank, such as the Federal Reserve Board in the U.S., in order to control inflation and stabilize currency.

Money: A medium of exchange, a good that can be used to buy other goods and services.

Money Market Deposit Accounts (MMDA): An MMDA is an interest-bearing account that allows you to write checks. It usually pays a higher rate of interest than a checking or savings account. MMDAs often require a higher minimum balance, and you are limited to only three checks per month. Most institutions impose fees on MMDAs.

Movement: The moving of people, ideas, information and products around the world.

Multicultural: A social or educational theory that encourages interest in many cultures within a society rather than in only a mainstream culture.

Muslim also Moslem: A believer in or adherent of Islam

N

NAFTA: North American Free Trade Agreement: The United States, Canada, and Mexico formed a major trading block in 1992 that removed tariffs and other barriers to the creation of a free trade zone among the three countries.

Narratives: In social studies narratives are stories or tales about events that identify the people involved, describe the setting, and sequences the important events.

Nation: A culturally and politically unified group of people bound together by a strong sense of shared values, institutions and cultural characteristics.

National interests: A perspective that puts the well-being of the nation before any other consideration.

Nationalism: The belief that nations will benefit from acting independently rather than collectively, emphasizing national rather than international goals.

NATO: North Atlantic Treaty Organization founded in 1948 to curb communist expansion. There are nineteen member countries of NATO, the North Atlantic Treaty Organization. They are: Belgium, Canada, Czech Republic, Denmark, France, Germany, Greece, Hungary, Iceland, Italy, Luxembourg, Netherlands, Norway, Poland, Portugal, Spain, Turkey, United Kingdom, and United States.

Natural/Physical Characteristics of Place: A description of "what is there naturally," the gifts of nature, such as water, minerals, land and timber.

Natural Resources: Anything from the natural environment that people use to meet their needs. They are "gifts of nature" that are present without human intervention.

Needs: Those things that everyone must have to survive.

Negotiate: To arrange for or bring about through conference, discussion, and compromise.

NGO: A non-governmental organization (NGO) is any non-profit, voluntary citizens' group, which is organized on a local, national or international level. NGOs perform a variety of services and humanitarian functions, bring citizens' concerns to governments, monitor policies and encourage political participation at the community level, e.g. the Red Cross.

Nonrenewable resource: A finite resource that cannot be replaced once it is used e.g., petroleum, minerals

Northwest Ordinance: In 1787 Congress set up a government for the Northwest Territory and outlawed slavery there. It also provided for the vast region to be divided into three to five separate territories in the future.

O

Ocean: The entire body of salt water that covers more than 70 percent of the earth's surface and is separated by the continents; and whose principal divisions include the Atlantic, Pacific, Indian, Arctic, and Antarctic oceans.

Oligarchy: A government controlled by a small group to serve their own purposes.

OPEC: The Organization of Petroleum Exporting Countries is an international cartel of thirteen nations designed to promote collective pricing of petroleum, unified marketing policies, and regulation of petroleum extraction.

Opportunity Cost: The next best alternative that must be given up when a choice is made. Not all alternatives, just the next best choice.

Ownership: The right to use something and to enjoy its benefits.

Ozone: A gas formed from an interaction between oxygen and sunlight

Ozone Layer: A region in the earth's upper atmosphere that protects life beneath by filtering out dangerous ultraviolet solar radiation

P

Parliamentary System: A system of government in which power is concentrated in a legislature. The legislature selects one of its members, usually called a prime minister, as the nations' principal leader and other legislative members deserve as the leader's cabinet.

Partisan: A fervent, sometimes militant supporter or proponent of a party, cause, faction, person, or idea.

Patriotism: Virtuous citizens display a devotion to their country in words and deeds, including devotion to the fundamental values and principles upon which it depends.

Per Capita Income: The average income per person.

Personality: relatively stable pattern of behavior and thinking manifested in interactions with self and others.

Personal Virtue: Moral excellence, the consistent practice of moral action and the abstinence from immorality and vices.

Physical Features: Natural characteristics of the earth's surface such as land forms, climate, winds, and ocean currents.

Physical/natural characteristics of place: The natural environment of a place such as water, minerals, land, and timber.

Pie chart: Used to display data that adds up to 100%

Place: A particular city, village, or area with distinctive physical and human characteristics that distinguishes it from other places.

Plains: Landform feature characterized by gentle slopes and minimum of local relief.

Plateau: Landform features characterized by high elevation and gentle upland slopes (e.g., the Grand Canyon area of the United States.

Platform: A formal declaration of the principles on which a group, such as a political party, makes its appeal to the public.

Plank: One of the articles or ideas of a political platform

Plessy v. Ferguson (1896): The court ruled that segregation was legal so long as facilities for blacks and whites were equal.

Political Freedom: The right to participate freely in the political process choose and remove public officials, to be governed under a rule of law; the right to a free flow of information and ideas, open debate and right of assembly.

Popular sovereignty: The citizens are collectively the sovereign of the state and hold the ultimate authority over public officials and their policies.

Population: The people who inhabit a political entity or region.

Population: A group of individuals which interbreed or exchange genes primarily with each other, and thus share traits in common more than with members of other populations. If a population becomes split, as from migration, so that one part no longer interbreeds with the other, gradually each separated group could accumulate changes not shared with the other and would thus develop or evolve into distinctive populations.

Population density: The number of individuals occupying an area derived from dividing the number of people by the area they occupy (e.g., 2,000 people divided by ten square miles – 200 people per square mile).

Populism: A political philosophy supporting the rights and power of the people in their struggle against the privileged elite. In U.S. History the populist movement first gains national importance in the presidential election of 1892. Agrarian reform and issues regarding bimetallism are cornerstones of the movement.

Preamble: Introduction to a formal document that explains its purpose.

Precedent: A judicial decision that may be used as a standard in subsequent similar cases: a landmark decision that set a legal precedent.

Prejudice: Holding unreasonable preconceived judgments or convictions especially pertaining to irrational suspicion or hatred of a particular group, race, or religion.

Presidential System /American Political System: A system of government in which the legislative and executive branches operate independently of each other and in which power in branches operate independently of each other and in which power is distributed through a system of checks and balances.

Price: The amounts of money that people pay in exchange for a unit of a particular good or service.

Primary Source Documents: Original documents that help us learn about past people or events (e.g., letters, diaries, maps, drawings, laws, statutes,).

Primary Sources: Any document or artifacts that is direct evidence of historical events including clothing, furniture, homes, recordings, documents and photographs.

Privacy: The state of being free from unsanctioned intrusion.

Private Goods: Goods that are privately owned and used to benefit only their owners.

Private Life: Concerns the personal life of the individual such as being with family and friends or practicing ones own religious beliefs.

Process: A series of gradual changes bringing about a result.

Processes: The series of changes by which something develops (major world processes are population growth, economic development, urbanization, resource use, international trade, global communication, and environmental impact.)

Producers: People who use resources to make goods and services.

Production: The act of growing, making or manufacturing goods and services.

Productivity: The amount of output per unit of input.

Profit: The positive gain from an investment or business operation after subtracting for all expenses. Opposite of loss

Propaganda: The systematic spreading of ideas or beliefs reflecting the views and interests of those advocating a doctrine or cause.

Property: That which is legally owned by an individual or entity.

Property taxes: Taxes paid by households and businesses on land and buildings.

Public Goods: Goods and services that are provided by the government. They are often too expensive or not practical to be obtained by individuals.

Public Policy: Decisions and laws that a government makes about an area of public concern to guide the actions of government.

Public policy issue (should questions): An issue about which reasonable people will disagree. Questions of public policy require individuals in authority to make decisions or create policies that will affect the public lives of all the citizens in a community or nation.

Public Service: Service to local, state, or national communities through appointed or elected office.

Pull factors: In migration theory, the social, political, economic, and environmental attractions of new areas that draw people away from their previous location.

Pursuit of Happiness: The right of citizens in the American constitutional democracy to attempt to attain – "to pursue" –happiness in their own way, so long as they do not infringe upon rights of others

Push factors: In migration theory, the social, political, economic and environmental forces that drive people from their previous location to search for new ones.

R

Race: Commonly used to refer to regional human populations assumed to be significantly genetically different from each other, though in the same species. Anthropologists hold that this view ignores the vast amount of genetic diversity within any population and the minimal importance of differences between populations, so that race is used to refer to ethnic group (cultural) differences as though they had a biological basis. Recent DNA research shows that the amount of DNA variation within any population is more than 16 times greater than DNA differences between populations.

Racism: An irrational belief in an advocacy of the superiority of a given group, people, or nation.

Reapportionment: The number of representatives in Congress is fixed. The Supreme Court has established that all election districts must be equal or nearly equal in population. States which must make changes as a result of new census figures (situations where new districts are drawn or seats lost---reapportioning) often experience rancorous debate by the political parties. Reapportionment plans can affect the ease with which a party can get its candidates elected.

Rebate: A partial refund following a purchase.

Reciprocity: Mutual exchange, especially an exchange of special privileges in regard to trade between two countries.

Reconstruction: Period after the Civil War when the south was re-built; also, the Federal program to rebuild it.

Referendum: The submission of a proposed public measure or actual statute to a direct popular vote.

Reform: Movement to improve unsatisfactory conditions.

Region: An area that shares common characteristics. Regions can be physical regions; land formations and climate; human traits that make up a region such as language, religion history and political boundaries.

Relative Location: Describes where a place is in relation to other places.

Relative Price: The price of one good or service compared to the prices of others goods

and services.

Religion: A personal or institutionalized system grounded in such belief and worship.

Religious Liberty: There shall be full freedom of conscience for people of all faiths or none. Religious liberty is considered to be a natural inalienable right that must always be beyond the power of the state to confer or remove. Religious liberty includes the right to freely practice any religion or no religion without governmental coercion or control.

Representative Democracy: A system of government in which the people choose political leaders to make policy decisions on their behalf.

Republic: A republic is a sovereign state in which all segments of society are enfranchised and in which the state's power is constitutionally limited. A republic is distinguished from a true democracy in that the republic operates through a representative assembly chosen by the citizenry, while in a democracy the populace participates directly in governmental affairs.

Resources: All natural, human and man-made aids to the production of goods and services. Also called productive resources.

Rule of Law: Principle that every member of a society, even a ruler, must follow the law.

Rural: Areas of low population density

S

Sales Taxes: Taxes paid by the consumer on the goods and services people buy.

Savings Accounts: With savings accounts you can make withdrawals, although the number you can make each month may be limited. Savings accounts usually earn interest. Institutions may assess various fees on savings accounts, such as minimum balance fees.

Scale: On maps the relationship or ratio between a linear measurement on a map and the corresponding distance on Earth's surface. For example, the scale 1:1,000,000 means one unit (mile or kilometer) on the map and represents 1,000,000 similar units on Earth's surface. Also refers to the size of places or regions being studied.

Scarcity: The condition that occurs because people's wants and needs are unlimited, while the resources needed to produce goods and services to meet these wants and needs are limited.

Secondary Sources: Summaries and interpretations of original artifacts.

Segregation: The policy or practice of separating people of different races, classes, or ethnic groups, as in schools, housing, and public or commercial facilities, especially as a form of discrimination

Separation of Powers: The distribution of political power among the branches of government, giving each branch a particular set of responsibilities.

Services: An intangible act, which satisfies the wants or needs of consumers such as medical advice and education.

Shortages: The situation resulting when the quantity demanded exceeds the quantity supplied of a good, service, or resource.

Site: The specific place where something is located, including its physical setting (e.g., on a floodplain).

Situation: The general location of something in relation to other places or features of a larger region (e.g., in the center of a groups of cities).

Sketch Map: The representation of all or part of the surface location on a flat piece of paper drawn from memory.

Slavery: The institution that supports the holding of human beings as property.

Specialization: The situation in which a nation produces a narrower range of goods and services than they consume/specialization in mass production occurs when a worker repeats a single operation over and over.

Socialism: Any one of various systems in which the means of producing goods are owned by the community or the government rather than by private individuals with all people sharing in the work and the goods produced.

Social organization: The rule-governed relationships of individuals and groups within a society that holds it together.

Soil: Unconsolidated material found at the surface of Earth, which is divided into layers (or horizons) characterized by the accumulation or loss of organic and inorganic compounds. Soil types and depths vary greatly over Earth's surface, and are very much influenced by climate, organisms, rock type, local relief, time, and human activity.

Sovereign: The person, body, or state in which independent and supreme authority is vested; such as, in a monarchy, a king, queen, or emperor---in the United States, the people.

Stock Market: A financial market which is organized to buy and sell stocks through exchanges, over-the-counter, and electronically.

Subculture: A distinctive set of standards and behavior patterns by which a group within a larger society operates.

Subsidy: A payment made by government to encourage some activity.

Substitute goods: Goods that can be used interchangeably. The consumption of one replaces the need to consume the other.

Supply: The quantities of a good or service that a firm is willing and able to make available for sale at different prices (economic concept of supply and demand).

Surpluses: The situation resulting when the quantity supplied exceeds that quantity demanded of a good, service, or resource.

Synthesize: Build a structure or pattern from diverse elements. Put parts together to form a whole, with emphasis on creating a new meaning or structure.

T

Taking a stand: Supporting one side of an issue of public policy.

Tariff: Tax on foreign goods brought into a country. An official schedule of taxes imposed by a government on imports or exports.

Taxes: Required payments of money made to governments by households and business firms.

Theory: A set of principle that can be used to make inferences about the world.

Three Basic Economic Questions:
1. What goods and services will be produced and in what quantities?
2. How will they be produced?
3. For whom will they be produced?

Timeline: A graphic means of displaying historical events in chronological order Tolerance - a disposition to allow freedom of choice and behavior.

Totalitarian: Country where a single party controls the government and every aspect of the lives of the people.

Trade/Exchange: Trading goods and services with people for other goods and services or for money. When people exchange voluntarily, they expect to be better off as a result.

Trade-offs: Giving up one thing to get something else.

Traditional Economy: an economy in which the three basic questions are answered by custom, or how things have been done in the past. Roles in traditional economies are gender based and often inherited. Barter holds an important position.

Treaty: A formal agreement between two or more states, as in reference to terms of peace or trade.

Trial: The examination before a court of the facts or law in a court case.

Trojan Horse: A subversive group that supports the enemy and engages in espionage or sabotage; an enemy in your midst; a large hollow wooden figure of a horse (filled with Greek soldiers) left by the Greeks outside Troy during the Trojan War.

Truth: A statement proven to be or accepted as true; in a democracy the principle that the government and citizens should not lie.

Tyrant: One who exercises absolute power without legal authority.

U

Unalienable: (also inalienable) Rights that cannot be given or taken away; that cannot be transferred to another.

Unemployment: The situation in which people are willing and able to work at current wages but do not have jobs.

Unicameral: A state government with a single legislative chamber.

Urban: An area characterized as a city or town where the population density is greater than in the surrounding area and is acknowledged as a major cultural, service, and production location in a region.

Urbanization: A process in which there is an increase in the percentage of people living/working in cities and towns.

V

Values: Beliefs of a person or social group in which they have an emotional investment (either for or against something); those things that are considered to be most important by a person or group.

Vigilante: One who takes or advocates the taking of law enforcement into one's own hands.

Voluntarism: People who work without monetary compensation to help others in their family, schools, communities, state, nation, and the world.

Voluntary Exchanges: Choosing to give one thing in exchange for another without being coerced.

W

Wants: Things that people desire.

Watershed: An area of land drained by a river and its tributaries.

Weather: Atmospheric conditions as regards to temperature, moisture, winds.

Wetlands: Productive land areas that are flooded for at least part of the year.

World Processes: Population growth, economic development, urbanization, resource use, international trade, global communication, and environmental impact.

World Trade Organization (WTO): An international agency which encourages trade between member nations, administers global trade agreements and resolves disputes when they arise.

THE **PARENT** COMPANION
A SUPER HOMEWORK DICTIONARY FOR PARENTS!

BONUS
TEXT LANGUAGE

a.k.a. Internet acronyms, text message jargon, abbreviations, initialisms, cyber slang, leetspeak, SMS code, textese

With hundreds of millions of people texting regularly, it's no wonder you've seen this cryptic looking code! Commonly used wherever people get online - including IMing, SMSing, cell phones, Blackberries, PDAs, Web sites, games, newsgroup postings, in chat rooms, on blogs, or on social media - these abbreviations are used by people around the world to communicate with each other.!

Acronyms have always been an integral part of computer culture, and they have since spawned a new language on the Internet. Commonly thought of as a series of letters that make up a 'word' there is a distinction between acronyms and shorthand. The actual definition of an acronym and text shorthand is here.

!	*I have a comment*
*$	*Starbucks*
**//	*wink wink, nudge nudge*
,!!!!	*talk to the hand*
02	*your (or my) two cents worth*
10Q	*thank you*
121	*one to one*
14	*refers to the fourteen words*
143	*I love you*
1432	*I love you too*
14Aa41	*one for all and all for one*
1Daful	*wonderful*
2	*to, too, two*
20	*location*
24/7	*twenty-four seven, as in all the time*
2B	*to be*
2B or not 2b	*to be or not to be*
2B@	*to be at*
2Bz4uqt	*too busy for you cutey*
2B~not2b	*to be or not to be*
2D4	*to die for*
2Day	*today*
2Dloo	*toodle oo*
2G2b4g	*too good to be forgotten*
2G2bt	*too good to be true*
2moro	*tomorrow*
2nite	*tonight*
2Qt	*too cute*
2U2	*to you too*
303	*Mom*
4	*for, four*

404	I haven't a clue
411	information
420	marijuana
459	I love you
4Col	for crying out loud
4E	forever
4Eae	forever and ever
4Eva	forever
4Ever	forever
4Nr	foreigner
511	too much information
53X	sex
5Fs 5	finger salute
747	let's fly
831	I love you
86	out of, over, to get rid of, or kicked out
88	Hugs and kisses
8T	it
9	Parent is watching
99	Parent is no longer watching
::Poof::	i'm gone
<3	heart
?	I have a question
?^	Hook up?
@	It means at
@Teotd	at the end of the day
A/s/l/p	age/sex/location/picture
A2d	agree to disagree
A3	anytime, anyplace, anywhere
Aaf	as a friend -or- always and forever
Aak	asleep at keyboard

Aamof	as a matter of fact
Aamoi	as a matter of interest
Aar	at any rate
Aar8	at any rate
Aas	alive and smiling
Aatk	always at the keyboard
Aayf	as always, your friend
Ab or **abt**	about
Abt2	about to
Acd	alt control delete
Ace	access control entry
Ack	acknowledgement
Acorn	a completely obsessive really nutty person
Adad	another day another dollar
Adbb	all done bye bye
Adidas	all day i dream about sex
Adih	another day in hell
Adip	another day in paradise
Afayc	as far as you're concerned
Afc	away from computer
Aise	as i said earlier
Aisi	as i see it
Aitr	adult in the room
Aka	or A.K.A. Also known as
Alap	as late as possible
Alcon	all concerned
Alol	actually laughing out loud
Alotbsol	always look on the bright side of life
Altg	act locally, think globally
Alw	ain't life wonderful
Ama	ask me anything

Ar	action required
Asamof	as a matter of fact
Asap	as soon as possible
Asaygt	as soon as you get this
Atwd	agree that we disagree
Ayce	all you can eat
Ayk	as you know
Aymm	are you my mother
Ayor	at your own risk
Aysos	are you stupid or something
Aytmtb	and you're telling me this because
B	be
B&e	breaking & entering
B&f	back and forth
B/c	because
B/w	between
B4n	bye for now
B4u	before you
B4yki	before you know it
B@u or **bak@u**	back at you
Baby	being annoyed by you
Bac	bad ass chick
Bag	busting a gut -or- big ass grin
Bak	back at keyboard
Banana	it means penis
Bbl	be back later
Bbq	bar-b-que -or- barbeque
Bbr	burnt beyond repair
Bbs	be back soon -or- bulletin board service
Bbsd	be back soon darling
Bbsl	be back sooner or later

Bbt	be back tomorrow
Bbw	big beautiful woman -or- big black woman
Bc	because
Bcbs	big company, big school
Bcnu	be seeing you
Bff	best friends for now
Bgf	best girlfriend
Bi5	back in five
Bio	bring it on
Bion	believe it or not
Bioye	blow it out your ear
Bioyiop	blow it out your i/o port
Bioyn	blow it out your nose
Bitd	back in the day
Bj	blow job
Buhbye	bye
Bump	bring up my post
Bw	best wishes
Bwdik	but what do i know
Bwi	but what if
Bwl	bursting with laughter
Bwtm	but wait, there's more
Byam	between you and me
Byki	before you know it
Bykt	but you knew that
Bz	busy
C	it means see, also a programming language
C ya	see ya
C%d	it means could
C%l	it means cool

C&g	chuckle and grin
C-p	sleepy
C-t	city
C/p	cross post
C/s	change of subject
C4n	ciao for now
Caac	cool as a cucumber
Cas	crack a smile
Cb	chat brat -or- coffee break -or- call back
Cbb	can't be bothered
Cbm	covered by medicare
Cc	carbon copy
Cd9 *or* **code 9**	it means parents are around
Chillaxin	it means chilling and relaxing
Chln	it means chilling
Ciao	goodbye (in italian)
Cico	coffee in, coffee out
Cicyhw	can i copy your home work
Cld	it means cold
Cm	call me
Cmb	call me back
Cmf	count my fingers
Cmiw	correct me if i'm wrong
Cmu	crack me up
Cnp	continued in next post
Cob	close of business
Cobras	come on by right after school
Col	chuckle out loud
Coo	short for cool
Crbt	crying real big tears
Cs&f	cute sexy & funny

Csl	can't stop laughing
Csn	chuckle, snicker, grin
Ct	can't talk -or- can't text
Ctmq	chuckle to myself quietly
Cto	check this out
Cu	see you -or- cracking up
Cu46	see you for sex
Cuatsc	see you at the senior center
Cuatu	see you around the universe
Cul	see you later
Cul8r	see you later
Cula	see you later alligator
Cuns	see you in school
Cunt	see you next time -or- can't understand newest text
Cuol	see you online
Cupl	couple
Cuz	because
Cwot	complete waste of time
Cwyl	chat with you later
Cx	cancelled
Cxo	chief insert title here officer
Cy	calm yourself
Cye	check your email
Cyl	see you later
Cym	check your mail
Cyo	see you online
Cyoh	create your own happening
Cyt	see you tomorrow
D	dad -or- it means the
D&m	deep & meaningful

D2d	developer-to-developer or day-to-day
D8	date
Da	there
Damhikt	don't ask me how i know that
Dbd	don't be dumb
Dbeyr	don't believe everything you read
Dbmib	don't bother me i'm busy
Ddas	don't do anything stupid
Ddg	drop dead gorgeous
Def	definitely
Degt	don't even go there
Dem	them
Denial	don't even notice i am lying
Dese	these
Deti	don't even think it
Dewd	dude
Dey	they
Df	dear friend
Dfik	darn if i know
Dftba	don't forget to be awesome
Dfwly	don't forget who loves you
Dga	don't go anywhere
Dgt	don't go there
Dgtg	don't go there girlfriend
Dgyf	damn girl you're fine
Dhyb	don't hold your breath
Difbet	it means what's the difference between
Diku	do i know you?
Ditto	same here
Dityid	did i tell you i'm distressed
Diy	do it yourself

Djm	don't judge me
Dk	don't know
Dkdc	don't know don't care
Dl	down low -or- download -or- dead link
Dltbbb	don't let the bed bugs bite
Dltm	don't lie to me
Dm	direct message
Dmi	don't mention it
Dnbl8	do not be late
Dnc	does not compute
Dnd	do not disturb
Dqmot	don't quote me on this
Dqydj	don't quit your day job
Drcowoto	don't really care one way or the other
Drib	don't read if busy
Dstr8	damn straight
Dtrt	do the right thing
Dui	driving under the influence
Duna	don't use no acronyms
Dunno	i don't know
Dur	do you remember
Durs	damn you are sexy
Dusl	do you scream loud?
Dust	did you see that?
Dw	don't worry
Dw2h	don't work too hard
Dwb	don't write back
Dwbh	don't worry be happy
Dwh	during work hours
Dwi	driving while intoxicated
Dwpkotl	deep wet passionate kiss on the lips

Dwwwi	*surfing the world wide web while intoxicated*
Dwym	*does what you mean*
Dyfm	*dude you fascinate me*
Dyhab	*do you have a boyfriend?*
Dyhag	*do you have a girlfriend*
Dyjhiw	*don't you just hate it when...*
Dyli	*do you love it?*
E123	*easy as one, two, three*
E2ho	*each to his/her own*
Eak	*eating at keyboard*
El	*evil laugh*
Elol	*evil laugh out loud*
Em	*excuse me*
Ema	*e-mail address*
Embm	*early morning business meeting*
Emfbi	*excuse me for butting in*
Emfji	*excuse me for jumping in*
Emi	*excuse my ignorance*
Eml	*email me later*
Emsg	*e-mail message*
Eod	*end of day -or- end of discussion*
Every1	*everyone*
Evre1	*every one*
Ewi	*e-mailing while intoxicated*
Ez	*easy*
F	*friend*
F2f	*face-to-face, a.K.A. Face time*
F2fmail	*face-to-face mail*
F2t	*free to talk*
Fab	*features attributes benefits*
Faf	*find a friend*

Fav	*favorite*
Fawc	*for anyone who cares*
Fbocd	*facebook obsessive compulsive disorder*
Fcfs	*first come, first served*
Fcol	*for crying out loud*
Fdgb	*fall down go boom*
Ff	*friends forever*
Ffa	*free for all*
Fwb	*friends with benefits*
Fyeo	*for your eyes only*
Fyf	*from your friend*
Fyi	*for your information*
Fym	*for your misinformation*
G1	*good one*
G2g	*got to go*
G4i	*go for it*
G4n	*good for nothing*
G9	*genius*
G98t	*good night*
Ga	*go ahead -or- good afternoon*
Gafl	*get a freaking life*
Gas	*got a second?*
Gawd	*god*
Gbg	*great big grin*
Gbh	*great big hug*
Gbtw	*get back to work*
Gg	*good game -or- gotta go -or- giggling*
Gga	*good game all*
Ggn	*gotta go now*
Ggoh	*gotta get out of here*
Ggpbl	*gotta go, pacemaker battery low*

Ggy	*go google yourself*
Ghm	*god help me*
Gi	*google it*
Gic	*gift in crib*
Gidk	*gee i don't know*
Gigatt	*god is good all the time*
Gigo	*garbage in, garbage out*
Gn	*good night*
Gn8	*good night*
Gnblfy	*got nothing but love for you*
Gnoc	*get naked on cam*
Gnsd	*good night sweet dreams*
Goi	*get over it*
Gr8	*great*
Gtsy	*glad to see you*
Gws	*get well soon*
Gypo	*get your pants off*
H&k	*hugs and kisses*
H/o	*hold on*
H/p	*hold please*
H2cus	*hope to see you soon*
H2s	*here to stay*
H4u	*hot for you*
Hagd	*have a great day*
Hagn	*have a good night*
Hago	*have a good one*
Hak	*hugs and kisses*
Hand	*have a nice day*
Har	*hit and run*
Hay	*how are you?*
Hb	*hurry back*

Hbib	hot but inappropriate boy
Hbo	helping a brother out
Hbtu	happy birthday to you
Hbu	how bout you?
Hhh	hip hip hooray
Hhis	hanging head in shame
Hho1/2k	ha ha, only half kidding
Hhoj	ha ha, only joking
Hhok	ha ha, only kidding
Hhos	ha ha, only serious
Hi 5	high five
Hig	how's it going?
Hmu	hit me up
Hoic	hold on, i'm coming
Hot pic	hot picture, as in sexy or naked
Howru	how are you
Hoyew	hanging on your every word
Hp	higher power
Htnoth	hit the nail on the head
Hu	hook up
Hugz	hugs
Huh	what
I 1-d-r	i wonder
I <3 i	i love it
I <3 u	i love you
I h8 it	i hate it
Ibtd	i beg to differ
Ibtl	in before the lock
Icbw	i could be wrong
Icbwicbm	it could be worse, it could be me
Iccl	i couldn't care less

Idta	i did that already
Idtbbf	i deserve to be blown first
Idts	i don't think so
Idwtub	i don't want to upset you but
Igws	it goes without saying
Ihnc	i have no clue
Ihno	i have no opinion
Ihu	i hear you
Ihy	i heart you -or- i hate you
Iiabdfi	if it ain't broke, don't fix it
Iiio	intel inside, idiot outside
Iimad	if it makes any difference
Iinm	if i'm not mistaken
Iir	if i remember -or- if i recall
Ij	inside joke
Ijs	i'm just saying...
Ijwtk	i just want to know
Ijwts	i just want to say
Ikr	i know, right?
Ikwym	i know what you mean
Ila	i love acronyms
Ili	i love it
Ilmj	i love my job
Ilu	i love you
Iluaaf	i love you as a friend
Ily	i love you
Ily2	i like/love you too
Imml	i make myself laugh
Impov	in my point of view
Imr	i mean really
Imru	i am, are you?

Ims	i am sorry
Inbd	it's no big deal
Inmp	it's not my problem
Innw	if not now when?
Ion	index of names
Iono	i don't know
Iot	in order to
Iou	i owe you
Ipn	i'm posting naked
Irl	in real life
Irncot	i'd rather not comment on that
Iso	in search of
Iss	i said so -or- i'm so sure
Issoys	i'm so sick of your stuff
Issygti	i'm so sure you get the idea
Istm	it seems to me
Istr	i seem to remember
Iswc	if stupid were a crime
Iswym	i see what you mean
Isyals	i'll send you a letter soon
Ita	i totally agree
Itm	in the money
Itma	it's that man again
Its	intense text sex
Its a d8	it's a date
Iuri	if you are interested
Iwalu	i will always love you
Iwbni	it would be nice if
Iwfu	i wanna freak you
Iwiwu	i wish i was you
Iwsn	i want sex now

Iyam	*if you ask me*
Iyd	*in your dreams*
Iydmma	*if you don't mind my asking*
Iyfd	*in your freakinging dreams*
Iykwim	*if you know what i mean*
Iynaegbtm	*if you need anything else get back to me*
Iyo	*in your opinion*
Iyq	*i like you*
Iyss	*if you say so*
Iyswim	*if you see what i mean*
J/c	*just checking*
J/j	*just joking*
J/k	*just kidding*
J/p	*just playing*
J/w	*just wondering*
J2lyk	*just to let you know*
J4f	*just for fun*
J4g	*just for grins*
J4t *or* **jft**	*just for today*
J5m	*just five minutes*
Jad	*just another day*
Jam	*just a minute*
Jas	*just a second*
Jc	*just curious -or- just chilling -or- jesus christ*
Jdi	*just do it*
Jdmj	*just doing my job*
Jfi	*just for information*
Jhomf	*just helping out my friend(s)*
Jic	*just in case*
Jk	*just kidding*

Jm2c	*just my 2 cents*
Jmo	*just my opinion*
Joott	*just one of those things*
Jp	*just playing*
Jsu	*just shut up*
Jsyk	*just so you know*
Jt	*just teasing*
Jtlyk	*just to let you know*
Jtol	*just thinking out loud*
Jtou	*just thinking of you*
Jw	*just wondering*
K	*ok*
Kcco	*keep calm & carry on*
Kewl	*it means cool*
Kfy or k4y	*kiss for you*
Khyf	*know how you feel*
Kia	*killed in action*
Kippers	*kids in parents' pockets eroding retirement savings*
Kir	*keep it real*
Kiss	*keep it simple stupid*
Kit	*keep in touch*
Kity	*keep it to yourself*
Kk	*kiss kiss -or- ok*
Kmuf	*kiss me you fool*
Ko	*knocked out*
Kok	*knock*
Kotc	*kiss on the cheek*
Kotl	*kiss on the lips*
Kpc	*keeping parents clueless*
Kutgw	*keep up the good work*

Kwim	know what i mean?
Kwsta	kiss with serious tongue action
Musm	miss you so much
Mwbrl	more will be revealed later
Myl	mind your language
Myob	mind your own business
Myt	meet you there
N	no -or- and
N pic	nice picture
N-a-y-l	in a while
N/a	not applicable -or- not affiliated
N/m	nothing much
N/t	no text
N1	nice one
N2m	not to mention -or- not too much
N2mjchbu	not too much just chillin, how bout you?
Na	nice ass
Ne1	anyone
Ne1er	anyone here?
Ne2h	need to have
Nfs	need for sex -or- network file system
Ng	new game
Ngb	nearly good bridge
Ngh	not gonna happen
Nh	nice hand
Nhoh	never heard of him/her
Ni	not interested
Ni4ni	an eye for any eye
Nice	nonsense in crappy existence
Nidl	not interested, dislike
Nifoc	nude in front of the computer

Nigyysob	now i've got you, you son of a b*tch
Nimy	never in a million years
Nino	nothing in, nothing out -or- no input, no output
Nism	need i say more
Nitl	not in this lifetime
Njapf	not just another pretty face
Ntbn	no text back needed
Ntim	not that it matters
Ntimm	not that it matters much
Ntk	nice to know
Ntl	nonetheless
Ntm	not that much
Ntmu	nice to meet you
Nttawwt	not that there's anything wrong with that
Ntw	not to worry
Ntymi	now that you mention it
Nuff	enough
Nvm	never mind
Nw	no way
Nyc	not your concern
Ok	okay -or- all correct
Olo	only laughed once
Om	old man
Omg	oh my god
Omik	open mouth, insert keyboard
Oml	oh my lord
Omw	on my way -or- oh my word
Omwt	on my way too
Onid	oh no i didn't
Onna	oh no, not again

Onnta	oh no, not this again
Onud	oh no you didn't
Oo	over and out
Ost	on second thought
Ot	off topic
Oth	off the hook
Otl	out to lunch
Otoh	on the other hand
Otp	on the phone
Otr	on the road
Ots	on the scene -or- on the spot -or- off the shelf
Ott	over the top
Ottomh	off the top of my head
Otw	off the wall -or- otherwise
Ousu	oh you shut up
P&c	private & confidential
P/u	pick up
P2c2e	process too complicated too explain
P911	parent alert
Pa	parent alert
Pal	parents are listening -or- peace and love
Pans	pretty awesome new stuff
Paw	parents are watching
Pax	passengers
Pb	potty break
Pbb	parent behind back
Po	piss off
Posslq	persons of the opposite sex sharing living quarters
Potato	person over thirty acting twenty one

Potus	*president of the united states*
Pov	*point of view*
Pp	*personal problem*
Prw	*parents are watching*
Ps	*post script*
Psa	*public service announcement*
Pso	*product superior to operator*
Pth	*prime tanning hours*
Ptl	*praise the lord*
Ptmm	*please tell me more*
Ptoyed	*please turn off your electronic devices*
Ptp	*pardon the pun*
Ptpop	*pat the pissed off primate*
Pu	*that stinks*
Puter	*computer*
Pvp	*player versus player*
Pw	*password*
Pwas	*prayer wheels are spinning*
Pwcb	*person will call back*
Pwms	*playing with myself*
Pwn	*own*
Pwnt	*owned*
Pwoms	*parent watching over my shoulder*
Pwp	*plot, what plot?*
Q	*queue -or- question*
Q2c	*quick to cum*
Qc	*quality control*
Qix	*it means quick*
Ql	*quit laughing*
Qls	*reply*
Qotd	*quote of the day*

Qq	quick question -or- cry more
Qs	quit scrolling
Qt	cutie -or- quiet
R	are
R u da?	are you there?
R u goin?	are you going?
R u there?	are you there?
R&d	research & development
R&r	rest & rexation
Raebnc	read a enjoyed, but no comment
Rafo	read and find o
Rat	remotely activated trojan -or- remotaccess tool
Rb@ya	right back at ya
Rbay	right back at you
Rbtl	read between the lines
Rbu	rainbows, butterflies, unicorns
Rdv	reader's digest version
Re	regards -or- reply -or- hello again
Rehi	hi again
Reso	reservation
Rfd	request for discussion
Rfp	request for proposal
Rgds	it means regards
Rgr	roger
Rhip	rank has its privileges
Ri&w	read it and weep
Rimjs	really i'm just saying
Riyl	recommended if you like
Rkba	right to keep and bear arms
Rl	real life

Rlco	real life conference
Rlf	real life friend
Rm	remake
Rmb	rings my bell
Rmetth	rolling my eyes to the heavens
Rmlb	read my lips baby
Rmma	reading my mind again
Rmmm	read my mail man
Rn	right now
Rnn	reply not necessary
Rny	it means rainy
Rofl	rolling on floor laughing
Rotfl	rolling on the floor laughing
Rpg	role playing games
Rrq	return receipt requested
Rrr har har har *(instead of lol)*	
Rsn	real soon now
Rsvp	repondez s'il vous plait
Rt	real time -or- retweet
Rtb	returning to base
Rtbm	read the bloody manual
Rtbs	reason to be single
Rtk	return to keyboard
Rts	read the screen
Ru	are you?
Ru/18	are you over 18?
Ruh	are you horny?
Rumcymhmd	are you on medication cause you must have missed a dose
Rumorf	are you male or female?
Runts	are you nuts?

Ruok	*are you ok?*
Rus	*are you serious?*
Rusos	*are you sos (in trouble)?*
Rut	*are you there?*
Ruup4it	*are you up for it?*
Ru\\18	*are you under 18?*
Rx	*regards*
Ryfm	*read your friendly manual*
Ryo	*roll your own*
Rys	*read your screen*
S	*smile*
S2r	*send to receive*
S2u	*same to you*
Sb	*stand by*
Sbi	*sorry 'bout it*
Sbta	*sorry, being thick again*
Sc	*stay cool*
Scnr	*sorry, could not resist*
Sec	*wait a second*
Sed	*said enough darling*
Sep	*somebody else's problem*
Sete	*smiling ear to ear*
Sfaiaa	*so far as i am aware*
Sfete	*smiling from ear to ear*
Sfla	*stupid four letter acronym*
Sfp	*sorry for partying*
Sfx	*sound effects -or- stage effects*
Sgtm	*sounds good to me*
Shb	*should have been*
Shhh	*quiet*
Shid	*slap head in disgust*

Shit	sugar honey ice tea
Shmily	see how much i love you
Sht	it means so hot
Shwaslomf	sitting here with a straight look on my face
Sia	say it again
Sic	spelling is correct
Sicl	sitting in chair laughing
Sics	sitting in chair snickering
Sii	seriously impaired imagination
Sitd	still in the dark
Situbi	say it til you believe it
Sj	strong jaws
Slap	sounds like a plan
Smaim	send me an instant message
Smem	send me e-mail
Smh	shaking my head
Smim	send me an instant message
Smop	small matter of programming
Smt	something
Sn	side note
Snny	it means sunny
So	significant other
Sobt	stressed out big time
Soddi	some other dude did it
Soh	sense of humor
Soic	so i see
Sok	it's ok
Solomo	social, local, mobile
Some1	someone
Somf	sit on my face

Somy	sick of me yet
Sorg	straight or gay
Sot	short on time
Sotmg	short on time, must go
Soz	sorry
Spk	it means speak
Srlb	spoiled rotten little brat
Sro	standing room only
Srsly	seriously
Sry	it means sorry
Ssc	super sexy cute
Ssewba	someday soon, everything will be acronyms
Ssia	subject says it all
Stbx	soon to be ex
Stby	sucks to be you
Str8	straight
Suakm	shut up and kiss me
Swalk	sealed with a loving kiss
Swdyt	so what do you think?
Sweet<3	sweetheart
Swf	single white female
Swim	see what i mean?
Swis	see what i'm saying
Swl	screaming with laughter
Swu	so what's up
Syk	so you know
Syl	see you later
Sys	see you soon
Syt	see you tomorrow
S^	what's up?

T+	*it means think positive*
T2go	*time to go*
T2ul	*talk to you later*
T2ut	*talk to you tomorrow*
T@yl	*talk at you later*
Ta	*thanks again*
Tah	*take a hike*
Tam	*thanks a million*
Tap	*take a pill*
Tas	*taking a shower*
Taw	*teachers are watching*
Tayn	*thinking about you now*
Tbh	*to be honest*
Tbt	*throwback thursday*
Tbu	*thinking 'bout you*
Tbyb	*try before you buy*
Tc	*take care*
Tcb	*trouble came back -or- taking care of business*
Tcob	*taking care of business*
Tcoy	*take care of yourself*
Td&h	*tall, dark and handsome*
Tdm	*too darn many*
Tdtm	*talk dirty to me*
Tia	*thanks in advance*
Tiail	*think i am in love*
Tla	*three letter acronym*
Tlc	*tender loving care*
Tlk2ul8r	*talk to you later*
Tm	*trust me*
Tma	*too many acronyms*

Tmalss	to make a long story short
Tmi	too much information
Tntl	trying not to laugh
Tnx	thanks
Tobal	there oughta be a law
Tobg	this oughta be good
Tom	tomorrow
Tomtb	taking off my training bra
Toon	short for cartoon
Topca	til our paths cross again
Tot	tons of time
Toy	thinking of you
Trdmc	tears running down my cheeks
Tripdub	it means www
Tsb	tall, sexy, beautiful
Tsh	too stinkin' hot
Tsia	this says it all
Tstb	the sooner, the better
Tt	big tease
Ttbomk	to the best of my knowledge
Ttfn	ta ta for now
Ttg	time to go
Ttiot	the truth is out there
Ttksf	trying to keep a straight face
Tts	text to speech
Ttth	talk to the hand
Ttthtfal	talk to the hand the face ain't listening
Tttt	to tell the truth
Ttul	talk to you later
Ttyawfn	talk to you a while from now
Ttyiaf	talk/type to you in a few

Ttyl	talk to you later -or- type to you later
Ttyl8r	talk to you later
Ttyob	tend to your own business
Ttys	talk to you soon
Ttyt	talk to you tomorrow
Tu	toes up (as in dead)
Tvm4yem	thank you very much for your e-mail
Twd	texting while driving
Twhab	this won't hurt a bit
Twhe	the walls have ears
Twtr	twitter
Twu	that's what's up
Txs	thanks
Txt	text
Txtim	text instant message
Txt	msg text message
Ty	thank you
Ur	you are
Ur2k	you are too kind
Ursai	you are such an idiot
Urw	you are welcome
Urws	you are wise
Uryy4m	you are too wise for me
Utm	you tell me
Uv	unpleasant visual
Uwiwu	you wish i was you
Uwm	you want me
Ux	user experience
V	very
W's^	what's up?
W@	what?

Wfm	works for me
Wrm	it means warm
Wrt	with regard to -or- with respect to
Wru	where are you?
Wrud	what are you doing?
Wrudatm	what are you doing at the moment?
Wsu	what say you?
Wt	without thinking -or- what the -or- who the
Wtb	want to buy
Wtdb	what's the difference between
Wtg	way to go
Wtg4a\\%/	want to go for a drink
Wtgp	want to go private?
Wth	what the heck
Wtmi	way too much information
Wuz	was
Wuz4dina	what's for dinner?
Wuzup	what's up?
Wwy	where were you?
Wx	weather
Wycm	will you call me?
Wyd	what you doing?
Wymyn	women
Wyp	what's your problem?
Wyrn	what's your real name?
Wys	whatever you say
Wysiwyg	what you see is what you get
Wyslpg	what you see looks pretty good
wyt	whatever you think
Wytb	wish you the best

Wyw	wish you well
Wywh	wish you were here
X	it means times
X-i-10	exciting
Xlnt	excellent
Xme	excuse me
Xoxo	hugs and kisses
Xoxozzz	hugs and kisses and sweet dreams
Xtc	ecstasy
Xxcc	kiss, kiss, hug, hug
Ya yaya	yet another ya-ya (as in yo-yo)
Yaba	yet another bloody acronym
Yacc	yet another calendar company
Yaf	young angry female
Ycmu	you crack me up
Yct	your comment to
Ydkm	you don't know me
Ygbk	you gotta be kidding
Yglt	you're gonna love this
Ygm	you've got mail
Ygtbk	you've got to be kidding
Yiu	yes, i understand
Yiwgp	yes, i will go private
Ykw	you know what?
Ykwim	you know what i mean
Ymak	you may already know
Ymal	you might also like
Ymbkm	you must be kidding me
Yngbt	you're not gonna believe this
Ynk	you never know
Yolo	you only live once

Yr	*yeah right -or- you -or- your*
Ysan	*you're such a nerd*
Ysdiw8	*why should i wait?*
Ysic	*why should i care?*
Ysk	*you should know*
Ysyd	*yeah, sure you do*
Ytb	*you're the best*
Yttm	*you talk too much*
Yttt	*you telling the truth?*
Yw	*you're welcome*
Yy4u	*too wise for you*
Yyssw	*yeah yeah sure sure whatever*
^5	*High five*

A SUPER HOMEWORK DICTIONARY FOR PARENTS!

INDEX

A

Abbreviations 34
Absolute Value 192
Absolute Value Zero 246
Abstract nouns 86
Absolute phrase 57
Acid rain 288
Adapt 288
Addition 136
Adjectives 38
Adverbs 40
Algebra 188
Albert Einstein 226
Algebraic fractions 192
Allegiance 288
Altitude 288
A.M. 157
Amendments 266
Amino Acids 246
Analysis 179
Ancient History 289
Angles 183
Antonyms 67
Apparent weight 154
Appendix 67
Appositve 55
Apostrophe 107
Associative Property 192
Atomic number 246
Atomic weight 247
Average 193
Auditory Learner 9
Auditory learner input . . . 15
Avoid confusion 259

B

Bar Graph 290
Bases 247
Bibilography 76
Binary operation 193
Biography 76
Benjamin Franklin 232
Butterfly Effect 193

C

Calendar 291
Capacitance 247
Capitalization 46
Carbohydrate 247
Carbon Dioxide 244
Cardinal Directions 248
Carnivore 238
Catalyst 247
Cause and Effect 50
Cell 7
Centimeter 150
Chain of reaction 248

Characteristics 240
Chemical Reaction 248
Choice 294
Chromosomes 248
Civil Rights Leaders 249
Clause/Fragment 94
Climate 295
Clouds 236
Colon 104
Collective nouns 124
Comma 53
Common noun 84
Common Verb 64
Communication 296
Community 296
Compass Rose 296
Complexities of Learning Styles 13
Complimentary Angel 195
Composite Number 196
Compound Sentence 60
Compound Subject 61
Compound-chemical 247
Compound Word 62
Compound Verb 64
Concrete nouns 86
Conflict 297
Congruence 196
Conjuction 65
Consensus 297
Context 66
Context clues 67

Continent 298
Contraction 69
Culture 299
Currents 244
Countable noun 84

D

Dashes 106
Decade 300
Declaration of Independence 301
Decimals 73, 131
Degree of an angle 196
Democracy 301
Denominator 197
Density 249
Dictionary 81
Different Learning Styles   6
Diffusion 249
Digraph 73
Dimension 198
Dinosaurs 237
Distributive Property 198
Division 162
Diversity 303
DNA 249

E

Economic Development   304
Ecosystems 306
Elasticity 249
Electrical Current 249

Element 249
Energy 249
Enzyme 250
Equality 307
Equilibrium 199
Estimating. 140
Ethnicity. 308
Expanded Notation 171
Exponents. 137
Extinction 238
Evaluate. 308
Evaporation. 250
Even Number 199
Evolution 250

F

Factorization 200
Factor. 199
Fats 251
Footnotes 76
Force 153, 251
Fossil 236
Fractions 167
Frequency 251
Function. 200
Fusion 252

G

Gene 252
Geography. 313
Geometric Mean. 200
Geometric sequence 201

Geometry. 183
George Washington
Carver 218
Globalization. 315
Governor 314
Graphic Data. 314
Graphing 146
Gravity 152, 252
Greatest Common
Factor. 201
Greater than less than. . .201
Greenhouse Effect. 314

H

Habitats. 315
Hadrons. 252
Heat. 252
Herbivore. 238
Highest Common Factor 201
High Pressure 241
Homograph. 81
Homonym 81
Homophone 81
Human Resource 315
Hydrocarbon 252
Hydrologic Cycle 316
Hyphen 105

I

Ice Age. 242
Improper Fraction. 202
Ingeneous Rock 240

Integers 161
Intersection. 242
Inverted Subjects 124
Inventors 218
Inverted Subjects 124

K

Kilometer 150, 151
Kinesthetic Learner 10
Kinesthetic Input 16

L

Learning Preferences 22
Learning Styles 6
Learning Style
Assessment 24
Learning Style Inventory   27
Least Common Multiples 204
Linear 203
Long Division 165
Longitude 322
Lower case reference list 48

M

Magnet 254
Main idea 133
Map of the United States 286
Mass 152
Mass Nouns 8
Measurement 149
Metamorphic Rocks 241
Metaphor 115

Millimeter 149
Mitochondria 255
Mixed Numbers 205
Mixed Operations 138
Molecule 255
Moment 255
Momentum 255
Money 171
Multiplication 160

N

Needs 325
Neutralization 255
Neutrons 255
Newton's Third Law
of Motion 255
Nonrenewable resource 325
Nouns 83
Nucleous 256

O

Obtuse Angle 185
Ocean 326
Odds 205
Odd Number 205
Order of Operation 139
Ordinate 205
Organic Compound 256
Outlining 88
Ozone 256, 326

P

Paragraph
Parellel.................206
Parts of an Angle.......187
PEMDAS 139
Perpindicular...........206
Pie Chart..............327
Place 327
Place Value............173
Plants.................49
P.M. 157
Polygon 206
Potential Energy........257
Predicate...............93
Prefix 97
Preposition 97
Prepositional phrase.....99
Presidents.............283
Prime Factorization 207
Prime Numbers.........207
Probability.............143
Products 257
Proportions............207
Protons 257
Punctuation............101
Pythagorean Theorem...209

Q

Quadratic Equation 208
Quotient...............208

R

Race..................332

Radiation..............259
Radioactivity...........258
Reciprocal.............208
Reflex Angles 186
Referendum 333
Rock..................239
Rounding..............140

S

Scale 334
Scoring Procedures 30
Science Giants 216
Scientific Notation 210
Segregation............335
Sentence..............111
Slavery................335
Similie 115
States and Capitals 267
Stem and Leaf 145
Straight Angles.........185
Subject 117
Subject Verb Agreement 121
Subtraction............137
Suffix 125
Supplementary Angle....211
Supporting Details......130
Synonym 66

T

Tactile Learning Input 17
Taxes 337
Temperature...........259

Thomas Edison 223
Time 156
Timeline 337
Topic 130
Topic Sentence 129
Treaty 338
Triangle 212
Trigonometry 212
Trigraphs 75
Types of Rocks 240

U

Uncountable Nouns 85
Unalienable 338
Urban 339
U.S. Constitution 264
Unit 212

V

Values 339
Verbs 132
Verbs in Action 62
Verbs Phrase 132
Visual Learner 8
Visual Learner Input 14
Volume 155

W

Water Cycle 260
Weather 245, 340
Weight 260

Wetlands 340
Whole numbers 213
Writing Process 133
Writing Parts 133
Writing made easy 133

Z

Zygote 260